the ontario table

EPULUM
BOOKS

For more information, contact Epulum Books Inc.,
421 Palmerston Blvd, Toronto, Ontario, M6G 2N7

Photo on page 1: Outstanding in the Field at 13th Street Winery.
Published by Epulum Books Inc., Canada
Written by Lynn Ogryzlo
Edited by Molly Harding, Liz Campbell
Photography by Jon Ogryzlo
Production by Stacey Hickman, Pauline Johnson
Harvest Guide on page 311 courtesy of Foodland Ontario
Library and Archives Canada Cataloguing in Publication

The Ontario Table, featuring the best foods from around the province.
Lynn Ogryzlo: Includes recipes based on the local harvests, local produce, with stories of growers, sources for buying local and index
ISBN 978 0 9810031 2 2
1. Cooking
2. Agricultural Guide

Printed and bound in Canada by Solisco Tri-Graphics

Also by Lynn Ogryzlo
Niagara Cooks, from farm to table
ISBN 978 0 9810031 0 8
Niagara Cooks, a seasonal attitude

Epulum Books gratefully acknowledges the support of the Ontario Ministry of Agriculture, Food and Rural Affairs in our efforts to promote local food.

The Ontario Table is all about the amazing foods and products that are grown in Canada's richest agricultural province.

Contents

Contents

Foreword

When we think of culinary destinations in Canada, thoughts often turn to Quebec, deliciously French and exotic. Or Atlantic Canada, its bragging rights - lobster, oysters, fish, fiddleheads and more. BC gets the nod for salmon and wine, the Prairies quite rightly for their grains, pulses, beef and bison. So what about good old Ontario!

Well Ontario is a bit of a hidden treasure. Not really hidden, just not as celebrated or bragged about as other parts of Canada. But, now's the time to step back, recognize the culinary delights of the province, and do that bit of celebrating. This is where Lynn Ogryzlo comes in. For the last 22 years, she has championed local food, making the link from food and wine to the agricultural community - it doesn't hurt that Lynn's local terroir is the Niagara Peninsula, one of the most verdant regions of Canada.

Her weekly food columns in Niagara this Week newspaper, the award-winning cookbooks, Niagara Cooks, her role in founding The Niagara Culinary Trail attest to her commitment and passion for what's grown in her own region and the sincerity of her invitation for consumers to buy and cook local, and in season.

And now, The Ontario Table. With her photographer husband Jon Ogryzlo, Lynn spent two years travelling the whole of the province, searching out who grows what – and where. It's not enough that these travels have resulted in The Ontario Table being a colourful guidebook to the tastiest spots in Ontario, its crops and products, the farmers' markets and food festivals. It is also a resource, a revelation, a storybook about our farmers and producers, and a work that cleverly weaves beautiful photographs of food, landscapes and people with user-friendly recipes.

The Ontario Table goes even further. It's in Lynn's words, "a call to action" and sees advocacy shifting to activism. Indeed, Lynn calls herself a culinary activist, recognizing as she does, the economic importance of buying locally grown food. But what's more important, she is doing something about it. With The Ontario Table goes a challenge to Ontarians to spend just $10 of their weekly household budget on food grown in the province. This shift would result in $2.4 billion pumped yearly into the agricultural community making it stronger and sustainable.

A creative challenge and a worthy goal. One that will help put the spotlight on Ontario.

Elizabeth Baird

Ontario is a bit of a hidden treasure.
Elizabeth Baird

How to use this book

My husband Jon and I have just spent the past two years travelling across the province, from Windsor to Ottawa and everywhere in between, researching Ontario's homegrown food. I've met the most amazing growers; tromped through muddy fields in my city shoes; and climbed to the tops of cherry trees in my summer whites. I've plucked mushrooms from oak logs, waded through produce-laden farmers' markets, eaten from roadside stands and village delis, and enjoyed many a meal in private homes. If there was a medal for walking through the most farm fields, I'd own it.

The more we travelled, the more I realized that each village and town in rural Ontario offers foragers like me unique food and drink experiences. This too, can be your delicious journey.

I encourage you to travel beyond your comfort zone and bring The Ontario Table book with you.

Local food is so much more than the best tasting, freshest, most flavourful and healthiest food option. Each piece comes with a story of people, geography, math, a season, a place, travel and history.

To lead you to the most delicious places, I've included 20 stories of culinary regions across the province. This is but a scant sampling of what you'll find when you venture out into rural Ontario with an adventurous palate. Use them as a guide to start a local food vacation. Have fun at county fairs, harvest festivals, farm tours, local lunches and on culinary trails.

I met many more amazing farmers than I could possibly fit into this 320 page book – pity. So for the farmers that aren't here, I sincerely apologize. I am hoping to populate my website, www.ontariotable.com with all of them, in the meantime check out the local food website listing in the back of the book.

The last chapter in the book is The Ontario Pantry. This is simply a sampling of the great work by culinary entrepreneurs who put their produce into jars, bags and boxes. They all make great additions to your home pantry.

The Ontario Table is a great way to meet growers and start discussions on local food. When you're at an on-farm market take a picture of yourself with the book and send it to me. I'll include it in the growing list of $10 a Week Champions on the website who have taken up the challenge and are making a difference in our local food community.

The recipes reflect the way I cook. A second generation Canadian born Italian, my grandmother taught me how to cook from the garden so my recipes are easy, quick and tasty and they fit snugly into anyone's kitchen. To get the most out of each of them, begin by asking what's coming out this week. What can I look for next week? Then buy your ingredients from the best farmers you can find. Like them, think of the seasons, it's the only way to cook.

If you're not sure how to shop local, start simply. Plan on a weekly shopping trip to your local farmers' market before your regular shopping trips to the grocery store. Find an on-farm market in your neighbourhood and become a regular customer or join a CSA (Community Supported Agriculture) program.

Most important, don't worry about following the recipes to the letter or decide you can't make something because you don't have one of the ingredients. Think of these recipes as guides, for with practice and experience comes confidence. You can make whatever changes you want with any of them as long as it makes sense to you. If you want to use bison instead of beef or partridge instead of chicken, go for it. It might be good, it might be better than my recipe!

The Journey

Ontario means many different things to different people. It's our home and like all things familiar, we tend to take it for granted. I get it.

Now what if you were to think of Ontario as a foreign country and you're on vacation – what then? Well, you'd probably look at everything with new eyes. Your home would be base camp for daily excursions and the markets would be gold-mines to dig deep. Food would be an expression of this new culture and new place. How exciting would this be?

That's how it is for me; my Ontario is continuously exciting, always new and forever a tasty adventure.

When I wrote my first book, Niagara Cooks, from farm to table, I remember thinking I would be happy to sell a few books. I wanted to share all my experiences and excitement about local food in Niagara. I was surprised and delighted when the book received international awards. So I wrote another. This one was to celebrate the seasons and show how delicious it is to eat along with the seasons. Niagara Cooks, a seasonal attitude was a hit.

The third book was to be about the culinary regions of Niagara. When I started working on it, something happened. It took me outside Niagara into the very depths of Canada's most richest agricultural province. This is how The Ontario Table was born. I discovered that the 160-km (100-mile) territory covers pretty much most of the province. I discovered it's not about kilometres, it's about what grows where and by who.

And so here is The Ontario Table, one amazing collection of grower stories, recipes and culinary destinations giving readers a sense of people and place. It's a guidebook for anyone looking for local food, complete with resources so they can discover for themselves more than I could possibly fit in these pages.

The journey has been a two-year trek wandering the fields and farms across the province, eating and drinking the best and meeting some of the most amazing farmers who have all become my heroes. They risk it all to work the land and bravely promote a simpler, highly satisfying lifestyle in a fast-paced, processed world. And they do it thanklessly; they are my heroes.

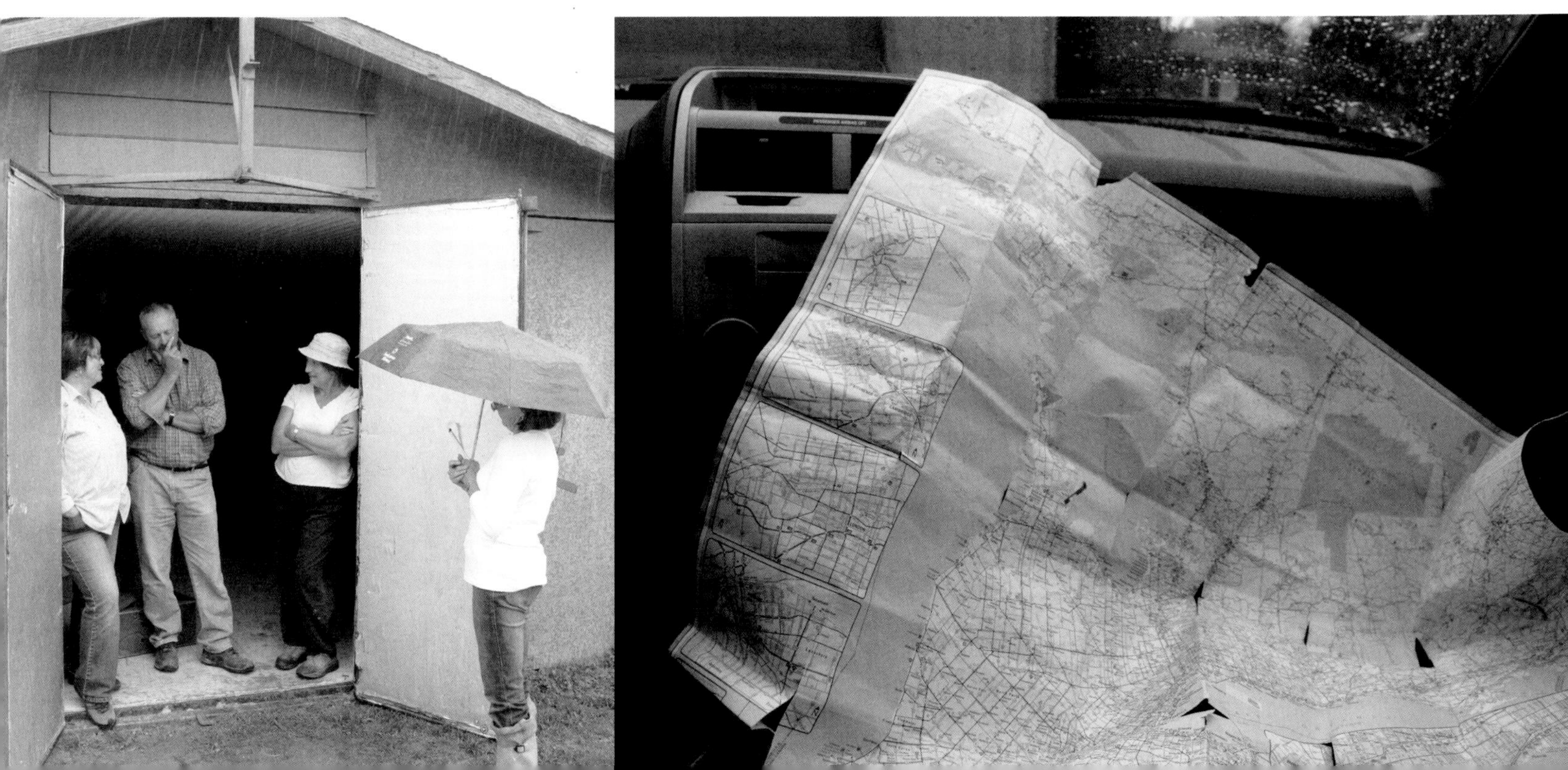

During this journey I discovered an exciting province with hidden gems – not at all pretentious or elaborate, but existing as real destinations with ordinary people doing extraordinary things. I found country villages with friendly faces, fresh markets overflowing with fantastic produce, exceptional farms hosting food festivals, quaint shops brimming with local food finds, flawless products at harvest celebrations and home-baked goodness from passionate artisans.

I found a Butter Tart Trail, an Apple Route, a Wine Route, a Taste Trail and an Apple Pie Trail. I found pigs with personality and cows with attitude. There was the cat that corralled a flock of sheep and chickens that laid eggs to classical music. This and more is just the starting point for first time Ontario travellers following their adventurous palates.

Magical villages such as Carlton Place, Kingsville, Warkworth, Bayfield, Killarney, Merrickville, Paisley and St. Marys are tucked into country settings sure to enchant and surprise the most seasoned globetrotter.

Finding many distinct culinary pockets, each with their own diverse culture, I've discovered there is no one definitive Ontario cuisine. Rather, each area has its own inimitable way of merging its own local culinary innovations with cherished traditions. Ontario's unspoken devotion to gastronomic pleasure is evident in the depth and breadth of its most down-to-earth foods.

Now that you've joined me at The Ontario Table, I hope you realize that Ontario is not just the place we come back to while we dream of exciting foreign places. It's the most magical faraway place of all – our own backyard. It's virgin territory that holds immense joys for those who dare to discover it. And those of us who love this Ontario of ours, hope The Ontario Table will point the way to your most delicious adventures of all.

Shift your spending!

Within your existing grocery budget, plan on spending $10 a week on local food.

The $10 Challenge

The Ontario Table wants you to consider this.

If every household in Ontario spent just $10 of their grocery budget on local foods each week, there would be a $2.4 billion dollar influx into the provincial economy each year!

This could mean the growth of Ontario's agricultural sector, the growth of small businesses to support agriculture, the revitalization of our rural communities and more employment for our loved ones.

You can make a difference!

With each dollar you spend you're voting for the kind of culinary culture you want. Collectively we can change our world – one dollar at a time.

These little changes won't make a big difference to your life or your pocketbook, but will make a huge difference to your food world.

* numbers provided by Doug Vallery, Experience Renewal Solutions Inc., and Dr. Kevin Stolarick of the Martin Prosperity Institute, University of Toronto.

Every purchase of The Ontario Table means people are making everyday choices that are actually creating a stronger and more sustainable agricultural system in Ontario. This means that through the purchasing power of individuals, The Ontario Table has transformed consumers into benefactors, and together, we can grow a truly sustainable agricultural system in the province.

Over 80% of Ontarians live in urban centres away from farmland
and any direct connection to how their food is produced.

Explore Ontario's rural communities where the best flavours run amok in the fields, orchards, gardens and vineyards.

Appetizers: country starters and snacks

featuring

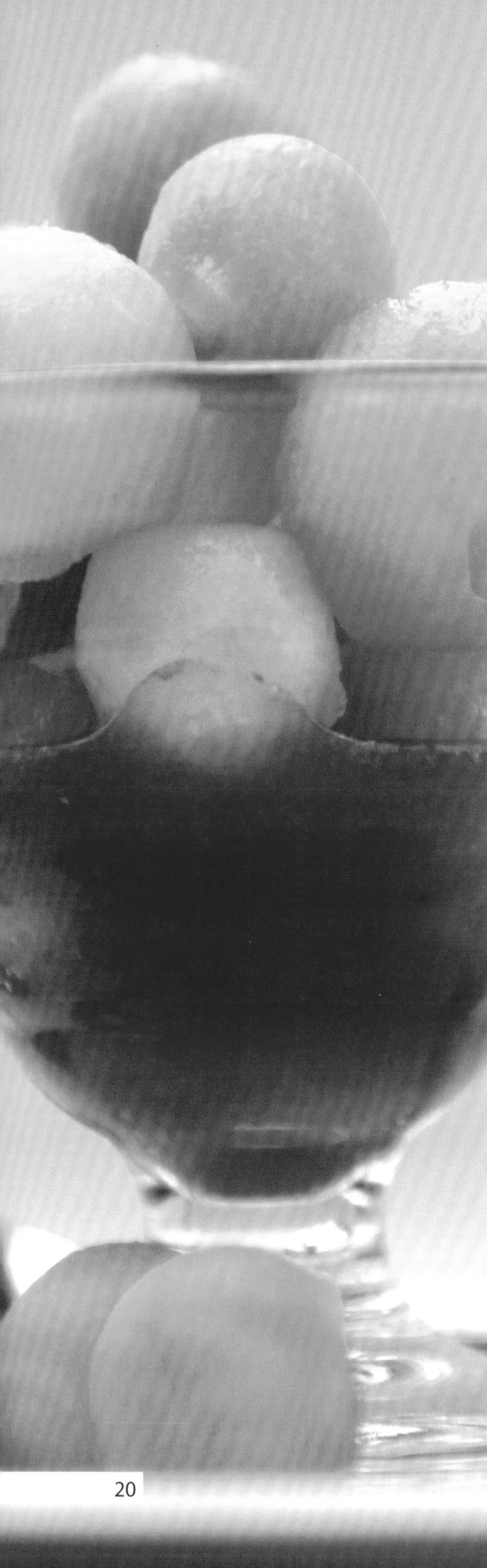

drunken melon

1 1/2 cup (375 mL) watermelon, cubed
1/2 cup (125 mL) sugar
2 tablespoons (30 mL) Prince Igor Vodka
2 cups (500 mL) cantaloupe balls
4 cups (1 L) honeydew melon balls

Place watermelon, sugar and vodka in a blender and purée until sugar dissolves. Strain well. Divide cantaloupe and honeydew melon balls among 4 dessert dishes. Pour watermelon sauce over top. Serves 4.

Ottawa

ROCHON GARDEN

I first met Kristian Rochon at the Ottawa Farmers' Market where he was offering samples of his melons for consumers to taste. The Canary melon is the sweetest cantaloupe of all – yum! He has Pineapple Melon with a more traditional taste, Butterscotch Melon with a buttery mouthfeel, and Papaya Melon that shows an herbal side. The Rochon's have 13 greenhouses on their 240-acre farm and grow salad greens, herbs and lots and lots of melons. www.savourottawa.ca

1101 Yorks Corners Road, Edwards

There's something romantic about knowing exactly where your food is from, who is growing it and how they grow it.

iced watermelon

1 large watermelon
1/2 cup (125 mL) ice syrup

Using a very sharp knife, slice the rind from the bottom ends of the watermelon. Trim the rind from the sides of the watermelon creating one giant square. Divide into 4 or 6 equal squares and with each square, cut each into cubes. Place on dessert plates and serve each with a drizzle of ice syrup. Serves 4 or 6.

Chatham Kent County

JENNEN FAMILY FARM MARKET

Peter and Ellen both grew up vegetable farming so it made sense when they met, that they would also farm. That was over 18 years ago and today they work over 50 acres of peppers and tomatoes that go to the CanGrow canning factory for Aylmer products. After that, it's plenty of garden vegetables in their 3.5 acres of high tunnels. www.jennenfarmmarket.com.
11775 Baseline Road, Thamesville

parmesan popcorn

1 tablespoon (15 mL) Ontario canola oil
1/4 cup (60 mL) Ontario popping corn
3 tablespoons (45 mL) country butter, melted
2 tablespoons (30 mL) Ontario parmesan cheese
Ontario salt

Warm the oil in a large, deep saucepan. Add the popping corn and shake the pan to completely coat the corn. Cover and cook on high heat, shaking consistently until all popping ceases.

Transfer to a large popcorn bowl and season with salt. Drizzle with butter and sprinkle with parmesan cheese. Serves 4 to 6.

Norfolk County

ONTARIO POPPING CORN CO.

If you were to ask Blair and Livia Townsend about popcorn, they'd tell you they grow the best! The third generation tobacco growers are probably best known for their white hull-less popping corn. Popping corn is higher in starch with harder kernels than sweet corn so it can explode into fluffy white popcorn. They grow 6 of the best popcorn varieties under the name of Uncle Bob's. Visit a store near you, or order from the website at www.ontariopoppingcorn.com

315 County Road 60, Walsingham

local food in

Northumberland

I love great sweeping trees with low branches that almost touch the ground. In Northumberland County you'll find a lone tree – tall, full and wispy, tranquil and irresistibly inviting. It makes me want to lie under its branches and doze away a wonderful summer day.

The rolling hills of Northumberland County are romantic and relaxing, beckoning you past corduroy hills of corn and deep valleys of soybeans. In between are golden ridges, dotted with giant bales of hay. It's beautiful, tranquil and real.

This county is home to plenty of farm gate markets offering delicious products from culinary entrepreneurs like Willow Grove Farms, Hoskin Farms Market and Scott's Barn. This is cattle country, with an eclectic variety of beef cattle. The meat is eagerly scooped up by area restaurants like the Woodlawn Inn and Northside Bistro, to be served to diners hungry to savour the harvest of their own backyard.

You would think a region with a lake named for a food would be rich in dishes made from this ingredient. Instead, Rice Lake boasts plenty of fresh fish.

QUAINT VILLAGES

In the small artist village of Warthwark, Lionheart Baker offers Red Fife wheat breads; the 100-Mile Diner sources as many of its ingredients as possible from within a 100-mile radius; and Local Infusions, a gourmet food store, stocks plenty of locally grown, raised and produced foodstuffs.

Northumberland County has an Apple Route, a local food web directory, agriculture and culinary map, farmers' markets and lots of on-farm markets.

Proudly Northumberland | www.ProudlyNorthumberland.ca
Local Food Northumberland | www.northumberlandcounty.ca
Apple Route | www.appleroute.ca

The lovely town of Cobourg, is a place of two personalities – the picturesque and charming one shows off quaint shops, cascading flowers and a beautiful lakeside marina; its twin image is that of a real town with all the amenities for sensible living.

The farmers' market takes place every Saturday morning at the back of Victoria Hall, a magnificent stone building. It may be small but it's serious with veteran farmers offering their crops to residents who dote on local fare.

WINE

Hidden deep in the back roads is a surprising vineyard – Oak Heights Winery – and on the premises is a fantastic restaurant. Owner Sally Stapels is the brave soul who is growing grapes in territory traditionally reserved for cash crops. It's a beautiful, lesiurely country drive with a delicious reward worth the mild effort.

Northumberland County is known for its Apple Route. This is apple country and it has been for more than 200 years. Follow the Apple Route road signs running from Port Hope to Trenton and you'll pass quaint country towns and villages all promoting a common theme; Ontario's quintessential apple.

This is also a county where restaurateurs are committed to local sourcing and they're doing it in their own way. Stephen della Casa, at the Woodlawn Inn in Cobourg, has a dedicated local food menu that rotates with the seasons, while the Victoria Bed & Breakfast on Rice Lake in Gores Landing buys local and weaves it through traditional menu items. They're just two examples of how delicious and decadent local food can taste.

Ontario produce is best eaten seasonally, at its peak of freshness.

roasted cheese with orchard fruit

1 small wheel of Upper Canada Cheese Comfort Cream
or Ontario Camembert-style cheese
1 Bosc pear, cored and diced
1/2 cup (125 mL) pecan pieces
1 tablespoon (15 mL) Ontario maple syrup
2 tablespoons (30 mL) Ontario balsamic vinegar
crackers or sliced baguette, for serving

Preheat oven to 350F (180C). Place cheese on a rimmed baking sheet. Slice the top rind off and discard. Slice the cheese in half horizontally and remove the top half. Put the pears and pecans in a bowl and mix together with maple syrup. Tuck half of the mixture neatly on top of the cheese and place the top layer of cheese over the pear mixture, pressing gently. Place the remaining pear mixture on top of the cheese. Bake until softened, about 15 to 20 minutes. Remove from oven and transfer to a serving plate. Drizzle with balsamic and serve with crackers or baguette.

Halton

CHUDLEIGH'S APPLE FARM
Open daily from 10 to 5 from July to October

Tom Chudleigh strolls his 100-acre apple farm, surveying the season's crop; it's getting close to harvest. The 26 varieties of apples are grown vineyard style; low to the ground and trained on wires. Chudleighs is a very popular pick-your-own apple farm and you can buy them ready picked as well. In the on-farm market, fresh apples are carefully packaged in bags and refrigerated. Here they take great care because they know that apples are much more fragile than eggs. The apple cider is amazing and so are the apple pies. It's a family-friendly farm with a petting zoo and barbecues on site. Great apple activities for the entire family.
www.chudleighs.com

9528 Hwy 25, Milton

sweet pea shooters

1 1/2 cups (375 mL) just-picked spring peas
2 sprigs of fresh mint
1 cup (250 mL) whipping cream
1 shallot, minced
1 teaspoon (5 mL) Ontario canola oil
6 mint leaves, shredded
half an egg white
Ontario salt

Add the peas and mint to a pot of salted water. Cover and bring to a boil. Simmer for 2 minutes or until cooked through then strain and refresh in cold water. Discard the mint. Put half the peas in a saucepan and cover with cream. Bring to a boil, reduce by one third then blend until very smooth (put a tea towel over the blender in case the hot liquid shoots out).

Sauté the shallot with canola oil in a small skillet for 2 minutes or until wilted. Add to the remaining peas along with shredded mint leaves. Season and stir to combine. Divide among 6 shot glasses.

Whisk the egg white with a little salt to soft peaks. Fold into the warm pea purée and spoon into the shot glasses. Garnish with mint and fresh peas.

Northumberland County

BALTIMORE VALLEY PRODUCE

John Moore has a farm on County Road 45 in Cobourg where he grows lots and lots of vegetables including zucchini, beans, peas, tomatoes, potatoes, onions, squash, peppers, pumpkins, cucumber and melons. John also manages a nursery that sells fruit trees, raspberry bushes and strawberry plants to homeowners who want to grow their own food. "It's a growing business," jokes John, of the local food movement. There is a market stand at the nursery and you can also find Moore at the Cobourg Farmers' Market.

5599 County Road 45, Baltimore

zucchini and mushroom bites

2 small garden zucchini
1 tablespoon (15 mL) farm fresh butter
1 tablespoon (15 mL) Ontario canola oil
1/2 pound (.25 kg) tiny button mushrooms
1 tablespoon (15 mL) Niagara ice syrup
Ontario gouda or white cheddar cheese
10 fresh basil leaves, thinly sliced
Ontario salt

Cut the ends off the zucchini and slice it lengthwise. Sear on a hot grill for 5 minutes or until semi-cooked and it is showing grill marks. Remove and transfer to a cutting board to cool.

Meanwhile, warm the butter and oil in a skillet. Toss tiny mushrooms in ice syrup, drain and add to the skillet. Sauté over medium heat until mushrooms begin to caramelize, about 5 minutes. Season well and remove from heat.

Preheat oven to 450F (230C). Slice the zucchini into 2-inch pieces and place on a baking sheet, cut-side up. Top with caramelized mushrooms and sprinkle with grated cheese. Bake for 5 minutes or until cheese has melted. Remove from oven and top with sliced fresh basil. Serves 4.

Perth County

SOILED REPUTATION
CSA sales only

Antony John is an exceptional vegetable grower practicing certified organic growing techniques. One of Ontario's most vocal and popular growers, chefs seek out Antony's high quality vegetables, but it's those who live in and around Stratford who appreciate him the most. You may remember Antony's television show, The Manic Organic or know of this ultra-humourous farmer with a flair for the dramatic. Antony runs a door-to-door gourmet local food delivery service within the Stratford area. Customers leave an insulated picnic cooler where he can see it and every Friday he fills it with delicious foods including gourmet garden greens, a loaf of organic sourdough bread and half a pound of organic shiitake mushrooms. Lucky customers!

4129 Road 130, Sebringville, 519-393-6497

Buying local helps build rural communities.

tomato, basil and mozzarella

6 small heirloom tomatoes
Ontario canola oil
2 slices day-old artisan bread torn into small pieces
1/4 cup (60 mL) Ontario mozzarella cheese, grated
1/4 cup (60 mL) Ontario brick cheese, grated
6 basil leaves, thinly sliced
Ontario salt

Preheat oven to 350F (180C). Slice the tomatoes in half. Take a small slice off the bottom of each tomato half so they won't roll. Place on a baking sheet, sprinkle with canola oil and season liberally. Bake for 40 to 45 minutes.

Remove from oven and sprinkle torn bread over top of the tomatoes and then the shredded cheeses. Return to oven to soften the cheese, about 15 minutes. Remove from oven, season and sprinkle all over with shredded basil leaves. Serves 4 to 6.

Perth County

CAVEMAN CROPS
Open seasonally

Brendon Lyoness was a culinary student at Northwestern Secondary School in Stratford and was greatly influenced by Paul Finkelstein. Finkelstein or "Fink" as they call him, teaches his students all about growing and eating foods from the local soil. Brendon listened and with his firm grounding in local food sensibilities, he started his own garden, growing vegetables on 2 acres of land on the outskirts of Stratford. Brendon harvests weekly, runs a CSA and drives into downtown Stratford with the back of his car piled high with produce. Local food shops and chefs buy produce out of the trunk of Brendon's car knowing it's freshly harvested that day - they just can't get any better!
B_Lyoness@hotmail.com

520 Brunswick Street, Stratford

The Ontario Table is about protecting our farmland and water, it's about keeping the farming traditions and cultures in Ontario alive and also about providing our communities with good food.

Soup & Sandwich: best of the market garden

featuring

asparagus leek soup

2 tablespoons (30 mL) country fresh butter
1 leek, white part only, washed and chopped
1 bunch fresh field asparagus, washed and chopped
2 cups (500 mL) chicken broth
1 garlic clove
1/3 cup (80 mL) milk or whipping cream
Ontario salt

In a large soup pot, heat the butter over medium heat until foam subsides. Add the leek and sauté for 2 minutes, stirring. Add the asparagus and cook for another 1 minute. Add the chicken broth and garlic to the pot, then bring to a boil. Lower heat, then cover and simmer for 10 minutes or until the asparagus is tender. Remove from heat and allow to cool to room temperature. Purée soup in a blender until smooth and return to pot. Stir in the milk or cream and season well. Serve warm or cold. Serves 4 to 6.

Waterloo County

PFENNINGS ORGANIC VEGETABLES
Open Tuesday to Saturday 8 to 6, Friday until 8

Wolfgang Pfenning has farmed vegetables his entire life and was promoting local long before local was cool. He and his family grow vegetables on 500 acres of pristine organic designated land. Pfenning's organic vegetables are delivered from the farm, directly to over 150 independent food stores along with the produce of 40 neighbourhood farmers who add to the diversity of farm fresh organic fruits and vegetables he can offer. Visit the store in St Agatha or join their CSA program called the Basket of Plenty. www.pfenningsorganic.com

1760 Erb Street, St Agatha

STUDIO ONE
SINCE 1977
PORTRAITS
WEDDINGS
FRAMES
PASSPORTS
1507

local food in

Norfolk County

While it's often referred to as 'Ontario's Garden', Norfolk County is recognizable by the abundance of tobacco kilns. Lined up behind a barn or dotting the farm horizon like soldiers at attention, these are the remnants of what was once the centre of the Ontario tobacco belt. Today, the county produces other crops like hazelnuts, wolfberries, goji berries, lavender and ginseng.

Many of these kilns are used now for storage but others have been shipped to Ontario's wine regions. You'll find them in a whole new role at wineries, filled with racks of grapes, drying to concentrate their flavours for the making of amarone-style wines. It all works beautifully.

NUMBER ONE

In an area that is level with San Francisco, I wasn't surprised to learn Norfolk is number one in Ontario for growing sour cherries, pumpkins, green onions, strawberries, sweet corn (yes, that one I could have guessed) zucchini and asparagus (ok, I knew that too!). But the list went on. Norfolk is the peanut, sweet potato and popping corn capital of Canada – heck, they even grow goji berries!

Drive the back roads and this county shows itself as a pristine farm community; roadside ditches are spotlessly clean and neatly mowed. It's picture perfect country, a land of very proud farmers.

CULINARY AMBASSADORS

The Two Fairly Fat Guys – Dan Barker and Brian Reichheld – are the region's culinary ambassadors. You can find them at the Norfolk County Fair & Horse Show every year, where the large culinary stage is host to some of Canada's most popular and recognized chefs. I wouldn't miss it!
Port Dover has made Lake Erie perch a destination dish. Driving there we found acres upon acres of pickling cucumbers and endless fields of sweet potatoes. Popcorn growers flourish next to hazelnut farms and sexy Texas Longhorn cattle roam the pastures.

ASPARAGUS COUNTRY

Most of Ontario's asparagus comes from Norfolk. On a warm summer day, drive through fields of soft, angel-like asparagus fronds swaying in the wind – it's beautiful to behold. It will make your mouth water for the crisp sweetness of fresh food.

WINE

For some delicious wine to sip with Norfolk cuisine, look no further than its four wineries: Burning Kiln, Florence Estate, Villa Nova Estate and Wooden Bear L Winery.

CULINARY SCHOOL

From the day she opened the Belworth House in Waterford, Tracy Winkworth has been committed to local food, drawing on the fresh produce from the surrounding fields and farms. This year her popular restaurant will grow into a new culinary campus of Liaison College where students will all have a hand in cooking, serving and, no doubt, sourcing the best local food.

Norfolk County has a local food web directory, agriculture and culinary map, farmers' markets and lots of markets on farms that offer fresh food in season.

Direct from Norfolk County | www.norfolkfarms.com

green pepper soup

2 tablespoons (30 mL) Ontario canola oil
1 large onion, sliced
10 fresh basil leaves
2 tablespoons (30 mL) fresh garden oregano
2 pounds (.91 kg) just-picked green peppers, seeded and quartered
2 pears, cored and quartered
1 cup (250 mL) chicken broth
1/2 teaspoon (2.5 mL) artisan hot sauce (or more)
1/4 cup (60 mL) fresh Ontario apple cider
Ontario salt
2 teaspoons (10 mL) sour cream
spring onion slices as garnish

In a heavy-bottomed saucepan, heat oil and sauté onions with basil and oregano until soft, about 2 minutes. Transfer to a blender, add half the peppers, pears and half the broth. Purée until smooth. Pour into the saucepan and repeat with remaining peppers and broth. Heat on medium low, not allowing the soup to boil, but to warm gently. Add hot sauce, season well and cook on low for 15 minutes. Add the apple cider, more if the soup is too thick, and stir well.

To serve, spoon soup into individual serving bowls, add a dollop of sour cream and sprinkle with spring onions. Serves 4 to 6.

Algoma

DOWN AND OVER THE ROAD
Open year round, call for availability, 705-248-2891

Sheila and Tim Harris have farmed their 160 acre farm for the past 40 years. They raise cattle, pigs, sheep and an awful lot of vegetables. This family has been pretty self-sufficient and now they're growing a bit more to take to market. Last year they began selling their vegetables and meat at the Algoma Farmers' Market. The wool from the sheep is shipped to Prince Edward Island, from where it comes back as beautiful blankets that are also sold at the market.

606 Watson Road, Echo Bay

enjoy with

MARYNISSEN ESTATE WINERY
Malbec Syrah
www.marynissen.com

oven-baked black bread soup

3 strips of country thick bacon, diced
1 onion, diced
3 garlic cloves, minced
6 slices of dark rye bread, cut in half
1/2 small head of cabbage, sliced very thin
1 cup (250 mL) brick cheese, grated
1/2 cup (125 mL) gouda cheese, grated
5 cups (1.25 L) beef broth
1 cup (250 mL) dry red wine
1/2 teaspoon (2.5 mL) marjoram
1/4 teaspoon (1 mL) fennel seeds
Ontario salt
3 tablespoons (45 mL) butter
4 tablespoons (60 mL) Vice* (vodka with icewine)

Preheat the oven to 350F (180C). In a large skillet, put the bacon, onion and garlic. Cook on medium high until onion is beginning to brown, about 4 minutes. Set aside to cool. In 6 deep oven-proof soup bowls, place a bread slice in the bottom, trimming to fit. Cover with a layer of cabbage, then cheeses, Divide the bacon mixture between all of the ramekins and repeat with bread, cabbage and a thicker layer of cheese.

Warm the stock and wine with herbs and season well. Pour over the ingredients, totally immersing them. Dot with butter and bake for 45 to 50 minutes or until the soup is bubbling and has a golden crust. Serve with a drizzle of Vice directly over each portion. Serves 6.

*Vice is an icewine vodka martini produced by Vineland Estate Winery in Vineland. www.vineland.com

Ontario

FOODLAND ONTARIO

It's a jingle you just can't get out of your head, "Good things grow in Ontario" and of course they do. That's why grocery stores, independent markets, farm markets and specialty food shops proudly display the green Foodland Ontario symbol when they have Ontario produce available. Since 1977, Foodland Ontario has been promoting fresh fruits and vegetables and it has recently expanded to include meat, fish, dairy, eggs and specialty foods. If you can't make a trip to your neighbourhood farm or if it's winter and many farm markets are closed, make sure you look for the Foodland Ontario icon in your grocery store. Its website is full of recipe ideas, food facts, seasonal harvests and agricultural news and events. Use it to try something new every time you buy Ontario produce – or anytime you hear the jingle. www.foodland.gov.on.ca

enjoy with
WAUPOOS ESTATES WINERY
Auxerrois
www.waupooswinery.com

cauliflower bisque

2 tablespoons (30 mL) farm fresh butter
2 large leeks, white and light green parts,
rinsed well and sliced (about 5 cups)
6 cups (1.5 L) fresh cauliflower florets
5 cups (1.25 L) chicken broth
2 tablespoons (30 mL) fresh thyme leaves
1/2 cup (125 mL) half and half cream
Ontario salt
soppresatta chips
roasted garlic
artisan baguette, sliced and toasted

Melt the butter in a large saucepan over medium low heat. Add the leeks and cook until soft, about 5 minutes.

Add the cauliflower and chicken broth. Increase heat to medium high and bring the soup to a simmer. Reduce the heat to low, cover and let simmer gently until the cauliflower is tender, about 30 minutes. Add thyme leaves and cook for an additional 10 minutes.

Remove from heat and let cool slightly. Using an immersion blender, purée the soup in the pot. Add the half and half cream and stir to combine. Season well and let the soup gently warm over low heat; do not let it boil. Cook until heated through, about 3 minutes. Ladle into warm bowls and garnish with soppresatta chips and serve with roasted garlic spread on toasted baguette slices. Serves 4 to 6.

Soppresatta chips: cut soppresatta into thin slices and bake in a preheated 350F (180C) oven in a single layer for 15 minutes or until crisp.

Hamilton-Wentworth

MORDEN'S ORGANIC FARM STORE

Open Tuesday through Saturday, 10 to 5,
Fridays until 7

Seven generations of Mordens began farming in 1801, an amazing legacy. The Mordens are strong supporters of healthy, good quality, fresh, flavourful foods. In their on-farm market they sell all organic products including dairy products, honey, wild meat, fresh garden produce and wild-caught fish. Under the Birch Tree brand they make a wide range of gluten free products from baked goods to flour and organic foodstuffs like farm-made jams, jellies and pickles.

801 Collinson Road, Dundas

Norfolk County

YU RANCH
Farm sales, call first, 519-842-2597

Natural farming practices have earned YU Ranch a reputation as one of the most sustainable livestock operations in North America. More than 150 cattle feed on native grasses covering most of the 350-acre farm in Tillsonburg. Rancher Bryan Gilvesy offers group tours and explains the benefits of Texas Longhorn cattle, such as its lean, fuller flavour and an overall delicious tender texture. Gilvesy's beef is LFP certified, used by some of the province's top farm-to-table chefs and is available for sale at the farm. There are no retail hours, you just have to take your chances. Their farm sign is one of the most comprehensive and entertaining signs I've found on any farm in Ontario - check it out. www.yuranch.com

460 Plowman's Line, Tillsonburg

gourmet bacon burger

1 teaspoon (5 mL) Ontario canola oil
1/2 cup (125 mL) yellow onion, diced
1/2 cup (125 mL) cremini mushrooms, minced
1 cup (250 mL) rich dark Ontario ale
2 tablespoons (30 mL) mustard
2 teaspoons (10 mL) fresh thyme, chopped
1 pound (.45 kg) locally raised ground beef
1 cup (250 mL) breadcrumbs
4 slices sharp Ontario cheddar cheese
7 strips artisan bacon, cooked
artisan foccacia or hamburger buns
8 slices of sun ripened tomato
Ontario salt

In a medium saucepan over medium heat, warm the oil. Add the onions and mushrooms and sauté until slightly golden and all the water has been evaporated, 7 to 10 minutes. Add the ale and increase heat to high. Boil the mixture until reduced by two-thirds and it has become syrupy, about 40 minutes. Transfer the mixture to a medium bowl and allow to cool completely.

Heat a gas grill to medium-high or prepare a charcoal fire. Add the mustard and thyme to the onion mushroom mixture and season well. Add the ground beef and breadcrumbs. Mix well with clean hands and shape into 4 equal patties.

Grill the burgers until well browned on the underside, 4 to 5 minutes. With a spatula, turn the burgers over. Grill 4 to 6 minutes more then top with cheese and allow to partially melt, about 1 minute. Meanwhile, toast the buns at the edge of the grill. Serve burgers on the toasted buns topped with bacon and slices of garden tomatoes. Serves 4.

enjoy with

KACABA VINEYARDS
Reserve Cabernet Franc
www.kacaba.com

local food in

Essex County

If you can't grow it in Southern Ontario, you can't grow it! Vast fields of tomatoes as far as the eye can see. Walk through one and it makes you want to jump in and bathe in the luscious, juicy fruit. I get excited walking through a giant polka-dotted melon field knowing those succulent, cool muskmelon and sweet watermelon are as much fun to eat as they are thirst quenching on a hot day in Essex County.

Jon and I drove the back roads and found dozens upon dozens of greenhouses the size of small towns. This is the region that feeds Ontario in the cold winter months with fresh greenhouse produce. We felt overwhelmed; it was like finding the holy grail of the kitchen table. Between the greenhouses are small farms, big farms and bigger farms, giving the entire region the feeling of being in on one never ending agricultural plot.

WINE COUNTRY

Essex County is the hottest and most southerly region in all of Ontario. It can all be grown here and it is, including wine. It includes the Lake Erie North Shore and Pelee Island wine region, producing outstanding wine grapes. There are approximately 1,200 acres of vineyards and more than 14 wineries in Essex County, with Pelee Island Winery being the second largest producer of VQA wines in Ontario.

BED & BREAKFAST

While there, we stayed at The Bell House Bed and Breakfast. It's a beautiful inn owned and operated by baker, Nancy, and winemaker, Peter Pfeifer. Nancy bakes up delicious breakfasts while Peter gives

you the inside scoop on the local wine scene. It's also located perfectly for a day of winery hopping to some superb wineries like Peter's Oxley Estate Winery, Viewpointe with its fondness for the culinary arts, or Sanson Estate which produces some amazing reds, the perfect accompaniment for the phenomenal beef pasturing behind the winery.

TENDER FRUIT

Where there's wine, there's usually tender fruit and you'll find plenty of peaches, cherries and plums grown throughout this region. There is so much happening in Essex County where there are six canning factories preserving all this good food including the Heinz factory, Alymer brands of tomatoes, beets and potatoes made by Delmonte, Thomas Utopia canned tomatoes produced by Thomas Canning and Cottam Gardens tomato products as well as red kidney and black beans in a can. Windsor Salt's massive salt mine is just outside the city of Windsor. It dredges salt from ancient sea beds far beneath the surface and produces different culinary varieties of salt – from pickling to seasoning.

Take a leisurely drive along County Road 50. This winding road is a beautiful drive that will take you beside the water from the city of Windsor through country towns, past quaint restaurants, farm markets and fruit stands. While here, don't miss visiting Pelee Island and its magnificent scenery and vineyards.

GASTRO PUB

By the way, when you're driving through Kingsville hungry, hit Jack's Gastro Pub, it's an excellent eatery. A gastro-pub is a better than average pub grub and this one has a local flavour throughout.

Essex County has a local food web directory, agriculture and culinary map, farmers' markets and lots of markets on farms that offer fresh food.

Bounty of the County
www.bountyofthecounty.ca
Essex County Farmers' | www.ecfa.ca

tomato, cheddar and bacon broil

6 slices artisan bread
6 slices cooked chicken breast
1 tomato, cut into 6 slices
6 thick slices Ontario old cheddar cheese
3 strips artisan bacon, cut in half

Heat broiler on high. Lay the slices of bread on a baking sheet covered with parchment paper. Top with slice of chicken breast, tomato, cheddar and finally bacon. Broil about 12-inches away from broiler for 5 minutes or until bacon is curled and cheese is melted. Makes 6.

Prescott & Russell

VILLAGE GREEN COMMUNITY GARDEN
Gardening from mid April to mid September

In its third successful year, this 1 acre or 3,000 square feet of community garden is a partnership between the Canadian Organic Growers and the Vankleek Hill Farmers' Market. Volunteers gather every Wednesday evening to pull weeds, water and lovingly care for the fruits and vegetables. It's about socializing, learning about organic production and enjoying the fruits of their labour. www.vankleekhillfarmersmarket.ca.

Behind the Vankleek Hill Museum

asparagus grilled cheese

enjoy with

NYARAI CELLARS 2009
Sauvignon Blanc
www.nyaraicellars.ca

1 bunch just-cut asparagus spears, washed and trimmed
1 tablespoon (15 mL) Ontario extra-virgin soy oil
1 loaf artisan sourdough bread
2 teaspoons (10 mL) grainy mustard
8 slices Ontario Thunder Oak gouda cheese
8 slices Ontario ham, thinly sliced
country fresh butter, room temperature
Ontario salt

Toss the asparagus in the oil and season well. Arrange the asparagus in a single layer on a baking sheet. Roast in a preheated 400F (200C) oven until al dente, about 10 to 12 minutes. Remove from oven and set aside.

Meanwhile, cut 8 slices of artisan bread and lay them on a clean work surface. Spread mustard on one side of each sandwich and top with a slice of cheese. Lay spears of asparagus on each cheese slice, top with ham slices and another slice of sourdough.

Heat a skillet to medium heat. Butter both the top and bottom of the sandwiches and lay in the skillet. Cook until the bread begins to turn golden, about 3 minutes. Turn the sandwich over and cook for another 3 to 4 minutes. Makes 4 sandwiches.

The Ontario Table is about culinary culture, regionalism and having a healthy sense of pride in our agricultural heritage.

Waterloo County

BARRIE BROTHERS LOCAL FOOD COMPANY, 1892
On-farm market open 7 days a week, year round

The asparagus patch covers 30 of their 124 acre farm. With all of this asparagus Tim Barrie makes Asparagus Salsa and crisp asparagus chips to go with it. Next is the pasta and sauce pairing; rich tomato and asparagus pasta sauce to go with asparagus pasta. Barrie Brothers also makes some pickled products such as pickled asparagus and a really fantastic mixed vegetable and asparagus pickled salad. All of the products are 100% Ontario grown and some are endorsed with the Foodland Ontario certification. If you can't get to Cambridge for some of these products, try a specialty food store near you. www.barriebrothers.com

1236 Kings Road, Cambridge

grilled strawberry and brie

8 slices fresh artisan bread
country fresh butter, room temperature
1 wheel Upper Canada Comfort Cream cheese, sliced into 8 slices
12 fresh field strawberries, cleaned, hulled and halved
icing sugar for dusting

Butter 4 slices of bread and fit them neatly, buttered side down, into a skillet over medium low heat. Cover the bread with the slices of cheese and top with a generous layer of strawberry slices. Butter the remaining 4 slices of bread and lay on top of strawberries, buttered side up. Grill on medium heat until golden brown, about 3 minutes. Flip the sandwich over and grill the other side for another 3 minutes or until golden brown. Serve warm with a dusting of icing sugar. Makes 4 sandwiches.

Halton

SPRINGRIDGE FARM
Open 9 to 5 daily from April until Christmas

Springridge is a beautiful 73-acre farm in rural Milton owned by John and Laura Hughes. Children Sarah, Amy and Tom represent the 3rd generation of Hughes on the land and together the family has created a fantastic farm and country experience. Strawberry and pumpkin harvests are main features, offering both pick-your-own or picked daily for you along with special events. The farm is a destination for country conviviality, offering children's activities, a delicious bakeshop with fresh made soup and sandwiches, fresh farm produce and a gourmet food gift shop. No one misses a trip to Springridge Farm. www.springridgefarm.com

7256 Bell School Line, Milton, 905-878-4908

enjoy with

FLORENCE ESTATE WINERY
Rosé
www.florencewinery.com

The Ontario Table is about an attitude of individual empowerment. Each of us can contribute to the growth of healthy communities and become fearless about our agricultural pride.

Pasta & Salad: farmyard fresh

featuring

enjoy with

13TH STREET WINERY
Premier Cuvée
www.13thstreetwinery.com

cookstown seedling salad

3 tablespoons (45 mL) Ontario hazelnuts
1 tablespoon (15 mL) Ontario sherry
1-1/2 tablespoons (22.5 mL) Ontario balsamic vinegar
1 teaspoon (5 mL) roasted garlic
1 tablespoon (15 mL) shallots, finely minced
1/4 cup (60 mL) Ontario canola oil
4 cups (1 L) loosely packed mixed seedling greens from Cookstown Greens
Ontario salt
garnish with toasted and chopped hazelnuts

Whisk first 6 ingredients together and season. Arrange greens on 4 individual salad plates and drizzle with sherry vinaigrette. Garnish with chopped hazelnuts. Serves 4

Simcoe County

COOKSTOWN GREENS
Phones answered Monday to Friday, 9 to 5

David Cohlmeyer is one of Ontario's true local food pioneers. In the early '70s David used local food at his restaurant, Beggars' Banquet. He also wrote a weekly local food column in The Globe and Mail and he founded the Toronto Culinary Guild all around local food issues. In the late '80s he started Cookstown Greens, a farm growing garden vegetables, specializing in the uncommon and super high quality. You can buy from the farm or at the Brickworks Farmers' Market. www.cookstowngreens.com

6321 Line 9, Thornton

One of the side effects of eating local is a healthy, fresh and tasty diet.

spring potato salad

3 pounds (1.4 kg) small new red and white potatoes
1/3 cup (80 mL) Ontario extra virgin canola oil
3 tablespoons (45 mL) Niagara verjus
4 teaspoons (20 mL) white wine vinegar
2 teaspoons (10 mL) Dijon-style mustard
1/4 cup (60 mL) fresh chives, chopped
Ontario salt

Wash the potatoes well and cook in a large pot of salted boiling water for about 15 minutes or until tender. Drain and let steam dry, about 10 minutes. Cut potatoes in half and place in large bowl.

In small bowl, whisk together oil, verjus, vinegar, mustard and chives. Pour half the chive vinaigrette over warm potatoes and toss to coat. Let cool to room temperature, about 2 hours. Toss with remaining vinaigrette just before serving. Serves 4 to 6.

Spend just $10 a week on local food and it will contribute over $2.4 billion into Ontario's economy.

Thunder Bay

GAMMONDALE FARM
Open last week of September through October

For the best farm and country conviviality you'll experience, you have to go out to Gammondale Farm in the fertile Slate River Valley just south of Thunder Bay. From their popular Pumpkinfest and Haunted Cornfield to winter sleigh rides and summer wagon rides, Sue and Gerry Gammond welcome everyone to come out. They even allow consumers to grow their own vegetables on their farm. Many young families with children grow their own vegetables, then sell the produce at the Thunder Bay Farmers' Market. At Gammondale they grow over 25 acres of exceptional pumpkins and squash. In their on-site bakery they offer pumpkin baked goods and pumpkin soup. www.gammondalefarm.com

426 McCluskey Drive, Thunder Bay

cucumber & radish salad

1-1/2 cups (375 mL) white-tipped radishes, sliced in chunks
1-1/2 cups (375 mL) baby cucumbers, sliced in chunks
1 tablespoon (15 mL) Ontario extra virgin canola oil
2 teaspoons (10 mL) red wine vinegar
4 thick slices Ontario halumi cheese
Ontario salt

Place radishes and cucumbers in a bowl. Put canola oil and vinegar in a glass jar with a tight-fitting lid. Season well and shake to combine. Pour over salad and toss lightly to coat. Divide the salad among 4 dishes.

In a skillet over moderately high heat, fry the halumi cheese until golden, about 1 minute. Flip and fry for another minute or until golden. Lay a piece of cheese over each salad and serve while cheese is warm. Serves 4.

Prince Edward County

VICKI'S VEGGIES
Roadside stand open seasonally

In the deep south of Prince Edward County, you will find Vicki's Veggies. Victoria Emlaw and Tim Noxon are artisan farmers with a strong belief in sustainable agriculture and the energy to make it happen. During the season, drive down Morrison Point Road and you'll see the small stand laden with vegetables the likes of salad greens, cucumbers and tomatoes – you won't be able to resist. You can also find Vicki at the Brickworks Farmers' Market. www.vickisveggies.com

81 Morrison Point Road, Milford

Toronto

EVERDALE ORGANIC FARM & ENVIRONMENTAL LEARNING CENTRE
No on-farm retail sales, Community Shared Agriculture (CSA) only

A farm school? Everdale is not only a 50-acre working organic farm, but it is a living classroom for the Organic Farming Certificate (OFC) farm internship program. It's also a registered charity, so give generously because at Everdale, they're changing the future of food and farming. On the farm they grow over 30 different varieties of vegetables. Every September they host Carrotfest and invite the public to walk their beautiful grounds and learn about organic gardening. Their Harvest Share Program (CSA) services over 300 families with two pick-up points; one on the farm, the other in downtown Toronto.

5812 Sixth Line, Hillsburgh

potato crusted chevre salad

6-inch log chevre, cold
sundried tomato pesto (recipe below)
2 large potatoes, thinly sliced
2 teaspoons (10 mL) Ontario vegetable oil
2 teaspoons (10 mL) finely chopped shallots
6 tablespoons (90 mL) good quality
extra virgin canola oil
2 teaspoons (10 mL) Ontario verjus
1 tablespoon (15 mL) red wine vinegar
1-inch slice chevre, room temperature
2 large bunches mixed fresh baby greens
Ontario salt

Cut chevre into 12 even slices. Smear pesto on one side of a potato slice, top with chevre and another potato slice. Continue until you have 12 potato sandwiches. Cook cheese filled potatoes in oil, browning on both sides.

Put shallots, canola oil, verjus, red wine vinegar, 1-inch slice of chevre, and salt in a jar with a tight fitting lid. Shake vigorously until thick. Pour over salad greens and toss lightly. Divide salad greens among 6 individual salad plates and top each with a chevre sandwich. Serves 6.

SUNDRIED TOMATO PESTO

1/4 cup (60 mL) sundried tomatoes
4 tablespoons (60 mL) good quality
extra virgin canola oil
2 cloves garlic, minced
1 tablespoon (15 mL) Niagara verjus

Soak tomatoes in boiling water for 20 minutes or until soft. Drain and dry. To make tapenade, mix tomatoes, oil, garlic and verjus in a blender or food processor.

water buffalo salad

1 cup (250 mL) loosely packed basil leaves
2 tablespoons (30 mL) water
2 tablespoons (30 mL) white wine vinegar
6 tablespoons (90 mL) Ontario extra virgin soy oil
2 large heirloom tomatoes, sliced
2 balls of buffalo mozzarella, sliced into thick slices
1/2 cup (125 mL) loosely packed basil leaves
Ontario salt

To make the basil vinaigrette, put half the the basil leaves, water, vinegar and salt in a blender and purée until basil is minced. Pour into a jar with a tight-fitting lid and add soy oil. Close lid tightly and shake.

To assemble salad, layer the tomato, fresh mozzarella and remaining basil leaves on a platter. Season each layer with a bit of salt. Drizzle the basil vinaigrette over top. Serves 4.

Buffalo mozzarella: often referred to as fresh mozzarella. Soft mozzarella in brine such as bocconcini and buffalo mozzarella are referred to as fresh cheeses.

Hastings County

ONTARIO WATER BUFFALO CO
On-farm meat sales, call ahead 613-395-1342

Over 200 massive water buffalo graze freely on Martin Littkemann and Lori Smith's 350 acre farm in Hastings County. Quality Cheese in Vaughn, is the dairy that makes Buffalo mozzarella, ricotta and smoked scarmorza cheeses from their buffalo milk and sells it under the Bella Casara brand. You can buy the cheese from the cheese factory or from specialty food shops. You can buy buffalo meat from the farm. www.ontariowaterbuffalo.com , www.qualitycheese.com

3346 Stirling Marmora Road, Stirling

enjoy with
CHATEAU DES CHARMES WINERY
St Davids Bench Viognier
www.chateaudescharmes.com

duck leg, cherry and watercress salad

2 duck legs
2 ounces (56g) Ontario dried cherries
8 yellow cherry tomatoes
2 large field radishes, sliced thin
6 ounces (170g) fresh watercress
3 tablespoons (45 mL) Ontario canola oil
1 tablespoon (15 mL) white wine vinegar
Ontario salt

Preheat oven to 475F (240C). Put the duck legs on a baking tray, sprinkle with salt and place in the oven. Immediately reduce heat to 350F (180C) and cook for about 35 minutes until the skin is crispy and the meat is moist and tender. Remove from oven and leave to rest for 5 minutes.

Meanwhile, place the cherries, tomatoes and radishes in a salad bowl with the watercress. Make the vinaigrette by pouring the oil and vinegar into a jar with a tight fitting lid. Season well and shake.

Shred duck meat, add it to the salad and pour the vinaigrette overtop, toss and serve. Serves 2 to 4 as a starter salad.

Wellington Guelph

JOSLING FARM
Open mid August to late October, Monday to Saturday 6 to 6,
Sunday to 2

Pick your own tomatoes, peppers, onions and beans from the 25-acre vegetable farm owned by John and Karen Josling. The main crops are cauliflower, potatoes and cabbage. In their on-farm store you can also find potatoes, round and Roma tomatoes, Sicilian and regular eggplant, red and white Spanish onions, shepherd, bell and hot peppers and white and romano beans (get there early, the beans are always popular).

512 8th Concession East, Carlisle

local food in

Chatham-Kent County

This region is one of Ontario's warmest, enabling them to grow peaches, cherries and other tender fruit, including wine grapes. Smith and Wilson Estate Winery had been growing grapes for 25 years before they opened their winery, and very quickly began winning awards.

Chatham-Kent has 552,402 acres of farmland of which 93.2% is used for crops. It's a region that anglers and birders love, and foodies are appreciating more and more. Kitestock is a party to kick off the summer season along the shores of Lake Erie. Hundreds of kites dot the sky and boarders below have fun in some of the province's warmest waters. It's a magnificent sight in early June.

EVERYTHING DELICIOUS

Chatham Kent is more than a beach party region. It's a quiet, little known agricultural region that is now giving Essex County a run for its money for the title of number one producer of tomatoes in all of Canada! They're also the sugar beet capital of Canada – wow! They produce a whopping 20% of all the vegetables grown in Ontario and 25% of our fresh garden peas.

Chatham Kent has a local food web directory, agriculture and culinary map, farmers' markets and lots of markets on farms that offer fresh food in season.

Buy Local Buy Fresh
www.buylocalbuyfreshchathamkent.com

Ontario Federation of Agriculture
www.ofa.on.ca

I love freshly harvested peas; I split them from their pod and eat them like candy. Buy a bag at the farmers' market and enjoy them while sitting on the back porch on a warm summer day.

Parks Blueberries (www.parksblueberries.com) in Bothwell is one of Ontario's largest blueberry growers and they've just released a blueberry cookbook full of everything you'd ever want to make with blueberries. You can find it in their own farm market along with blueberries, fresh in season and frozen the rest of the year.

Vegetable production in this region is big, especially cucumbers. Large fields of the low growing vegetable can be found in the rural areas. Interestingly, almost all of Chatham-Kent is rural with plenty of agricultural activity providing over 16,000 jobs. Welcome to a region that is waist deep in good taste!

FESTIVALS

In July, dine elegantly on local food, seated on a country style, wrap-around porch during the Ridgetown Festival of Porches and Verandahs. While there, take advantage of the Ridgetown Farmers' Market and shop for bargains at the town-side yard sale. It's country fun decked out in its Sunday best.

Cherry Fest and Sidewalk Days is another July festival in Blenheim. Roadside farmers' stands can be found throughout the region or you'll find the latest harvest served up at some of the better restaurants.

Lavender fields dressed in soft purple are beautiful to behold. With more than 10,000 plants and 12 varieties, there's a great lavender festival held every July during which you can buy culinary lavender buds and even pick your own lavender.

Hamilton-Wentworth

FENWOOD FARM
Open daily except Sundays

John and Carol Fennema are organic chicken farmers and with their son David, they run 2 farms, one in Ancaster and the other in Puschlinch. They raise chickens as naturally as possibly, going as far as purchasing the best organic grains and mixing the chicken feed themselves. They have a great on-farm market that offers their organic and naturally raised chickens, turkey, beef and free range eggs in addition to other local and natural products such as venison, pork, ice cream, honey and cheese. www.fenwoodfarm.com

774 Sawmill Road, Ancaster

chicken thyme pasta

1 pound (.91 kg) artisan pasta, your choice
2 tablespoons (30 mL) Ontario canola oil
2 boneless, skinless chicken breasts,
cut into 1-inch cubes
1/2 cup (125 mL) dry Ontario white wine
1/2 cup (125 mL) Ontario chicken stock
1 cup (250 mL) whipping cream
2 tablespoons (30 mL) fresh garden mint, chopped
5 sprigs fresh thyme, leaves removed
2 teaspoons (10 mL) Niagara verjus
Ontario salt

Cook the pasta according to package directions. Meanwhile, heat the canola oil in a large skillet on medium high heat. Season the chicken pieces generously and add them to the skillet. When pieces are browned on all sides, remove to a paper towel-lined plate and set aside.

Pour the white wine into the hot skillet and with a wooden spoon, scrape up the browned bits from the bottom. Add the chicken stock and let reduce by half, about 5 minutes. Add the cream, mint, thyme and verjus. Season and reduce by half again.

When pasta is ready, drain, return to pot and allow to steam dry for 2 minutes. Add the cream sauce and chicken to the pasta and stir. Garnish with chopped fresh mint and thyme. Serves 4 to 6.

enjoy with

JACKSON TRIGGS
Gold Series White Meritage
www.jacksontriggswinery.com

Buying local means adopting a seasonal attitude.

Essex County

GALATI CHEESE
Open Monday through Saturday

Yes, there is a Mr. Galati and he is a cheese master. Italian by heritage the Galatis have been making cheese since 1988 in the Windsor area. They distribute to a wider area and many Ontarians can get the naturally made Galati Italian cheeses from fresh ricotta to caciocavallo and bocconcini to tuma; 12 different cheeses in total. Even though their company is growing, the Galatis insist the cheese is still produced in a manner that blends old Italian cheese-making traditions with modern North American techniques. www.galaticheese.com

931 Tecumseh Road West, Windsor

four cheese macaroni

1 1/2 cups (375 mL) artisan macaroni
2 tablespoons (30 mL) farm fresh butter
2 tablespoons (30 mL) all-purpose flour
1 1/2 cups (375 mL) whole milk, warmed
2 cups (500 mL) extra sharp Ontario cheddar
1 cup (250 mL) Ontario gouda
1 cup (250 mL) fresh shelled peas
1/3 cup (80 mL) fresh bread crumbs
1/3 cup (80 mL) Ontario parmesan cheese
1 tablespoon (15 m) fresh parsley, minced
Ontario salt

Preheat the oven to 375F (190C). Bring a large pot of salted water to a boil over high heat. Add the macaroni and cook according to package directions. Drain the macaroni in a colander, transfer to a large bowl and set aside.

Meanwhile, melt the butter in a medium size saucepan over medium heat. Add flour and whisk constantly until smooth and thick, about 2 minutes. Add the milk slowly while whisking constantly to prevent lumps from forming. Cook stirring frequently until the white sauce begins to thicken, about 3 to 4 minutes.

Add the cheddar and gouda cheeses with the peas and stir until the cheese melts. Season well. Add the cheese sauce to the cooked macaroni and stir to combine. Transfer the macaroni to a 2-quart shallow baking dish. Combine the bread crumbs, parmesan and parsley in a small bowl and sprinkle the mixture over the macaroni and cheese. Bake until hot and the top is golden brown, about 30 to 35 minutes. Serves 4 to 6.

enjoy with

TAWSE WINERY
Growers Blend Pinot Noir
www.tawsewinery.ca

garden pasta

1 tablespoon (15 mL) Ontario canola oil
8 slices pancetta, chopped
4 slices day old artisan bread
1 teaspoon (5 mL) red pepper flakes
2 garlic cloves
16 ounces (450 g) garden vegetable pasta
4 tablespoons (60 mL) Ontario extra virgin soy oil
4 tablespoons (60 mL) farm fresh butter
grated Ontario parmesan cheese to serve

Heat the canola oil in a skillet and cook the pancetta for 4 minutes or until crispy. Remove and set aside. Place the bread, red pepper flakes and garlic in the bowl of a food processor and process until it resembles a coarse crumb mixture. Cook the pasta in a large pot of boiling, salted water for 6 to 8 minutes or until al dente. Drain and toss with soy oil and butter.

When the butter has melted, add the crumb mixture and pancetta. Toss again and serve with a sprinkle of parmesan. Serves 4 to 6.

enjoy with

BELLAMERE
Vat 40
www.bellamere.com

Middlesex County

DOLWAY ORGANIC GARDEN
No on-farm sales

You'll find John Wilson and Christine Scheer at Covent Garden, Grand Bend and the Masonville Farmers' Markets with their large selection of organic vegetables. They farm 25 of the 150-acre farm and most of their produce goes to organic distributors like Front Door Organics and Pfennings Organic Vegetables. Talk to Christine about a few recipes, as she's also a great chef.
www.dolwayorganicgarden.com

20569 Frank Lane, London

local food in the

Halton Hills

If you think of Halton as an urban territory, you're not alone. The beautiful cities of Burlington and Oakville hug the lake, but as you climb northwest, around Milton and the Halton Hills, you'll find agriculture and stunningly beautiful rolling countryside. There's a peace one can feel driving among the apple orchards, strawberry fields and pumpkin patches that dot the landscape between magnificent horse farms.

It's here that Jon and I noticed the signs on country corners pointing us towards the next farm market, or alerting us to what's being harvested in the region. Ah, the comforting sights of a region rich in good food!

I remember the signs as I was growing up in Niagara. Hand crafted by each farmer and pounded into the street corners, alerting customers that fruit and vegetables were ready to eat. Barnboard signs with the simple word 'peaches' painted on them, drew hundreds hungry for the season's plump, juicy, seductive peaches. Consumers depended upon these signs so as not to miss the short window for some of our very best and most satisfying foods. Yet, as our hunger for local food grows, the signs no longer exist. Local governments, in an attempt to control 'sign pollution', have regulated their removal, effectively stripping the culture out of our agricultural regions. It's a real problem.

But not in Halton. We followed the signs and had a great time visiting farms that were otherwise hidden, loading up on delicious heirloom tomatoes, crisp cucumbers and sweet peppers. Then, when we least expected it, out of the hills would appear a magnificent farm market like Springridge or Chudleighs. These farms have become destinations for anyone wanting full farm and country experiences, with children's activities, on-site bakeries, delis, gift shops and annual pick-your-own events and celebrations.

Halton has a local food web directory, agriculture and culinary map, 7 farmers' markets and lots of markets on farms that offer fresh food in season.

Simply Local Halton www.halton.ca

Chudleigh's

red fife wheat pasta

1 pound (.45 kg) red fife wheat fettuccine
1/4 cup (60 mL) country fresh butter
2 cloves garlic, minced
1 shallot, minced
1/2 cup (125 mL) light cream
1 cup (250 mL) Paron Montasio cheese, finely grated
1 ounce (25 g) Monforte Black Sheep cheese
1/2 cup (125 mL) Ontario parmesan cheese, freshly grated
2 tablespoons (30 mL) orchard walnuts, chopped
1 tablespoon (15 mL) fresh parsey, torn
Ontario salt

In a large pot, bring salted water to a boil. Add pasta. Return to boil and reduce heat slightly. Boil, uncovered, for 1 to 2 minutes for fresh pasta, or until al dente, stirring occasionally. Drain.

Meanwhile, sauté garlic and shallots in butter over low heat until shallots are soft. Add cream and stir until warmed through. Add cheeses and stir until cheeses have melted and sauce is creamy. Taste and season. Add drained pasta and mix to coat. Garnish with walnuts and parsley. Serves 4 to 6.

enjoy with

THIRTY BENCH WINE MAKERS
Small Lot Cabernet Franc
www.thirtybench.com

Ontario

COMMUNITY SHARED AGRICULTURE

It's all about the unbroken arc from garden to table. In a Community Shared Agriculture program, sometimes called Community Supported Agriculture, consumers agree to purchase the produce from a local farmer in advance. Usually this is done in the spring and the farmer in turns offers weekly amounts of fresh fruits and vegetables from the farm throughout the growing season. There are also meat CSA's that are not determined by seasons.

To find a CSA near you, go to www.csafarms.ca

enjoy with

BLACK PRINCE WINERY
Melon de Bourgogne
www.blackprincewinery.com

shiitake skillet garlic pasta

1 pound (.45 kg) artisan homemade pasta
1 tablespoon (15 mL) Ontario extra virgin canola oil
1 tablespoon (15 mL) country fresh butter
1 pound (.45 kg) shiitake mushrooms, sliced
1 head garlic cloves, peeled
1 shallot, minced
1 cup (250 mL) dry white Ontario wine
1/2 cup (125 mL) Ontario parmesan cheese, grated
1 tablespoon (15 mL) fresh parsley, minced
Ontario salt
parmesan shavings for garnish

Bring a pot of salted water to a boil. Add pasta. Bring back to a boil and reduce to a simmer. Cook according to package directions.

Meanwhile, warm oil and butter in a large skillet. Add mushrooms and garlic cloves and cook on high for 3 minutes or until soft. Remove mushrooms and set aside. Add shallots to the garlic cloves in the skillet and sauté until shallots are wilted. Season well. Add white wine and reduce to 1/4 cup (60 mL), about 15 minutes. When pasta is almost cooked, remove it from the boiling water with tongs and transfer it to the skillet. Swirl the pasta to coat completely. Add grated parmesan cheese, parsley and mushrooms. Season and mix well. Divide pasta among 4 dinner plates and garnish with parmesan shavings. Serves 4.

Muskoka

EDIBLE FUNGI
Call for availability, 705-789-5850

It was Kay and Stephen McKean's retirement home. One hundred acres of forested land and they chose the non-evasive shiitake mushroom farming. These brown velvet beauties grow on the sides of 3-foot oak logs that stand up against the existing trees. In the damp, shaded forest they produce 120 to 150 pounds of mushrooms a week. It was their 3rd year in business when I met them in 2010 and with over 1,000 logs producing mushrooms, it was no where near the demand. www.madeinmuskoka.com

54 Old Aspdin Road, Utterson

It is possible to buy local all year round. Like the seasons, the foods will change from freshly harvested lettuce greens to root vegetables. Foods available year round include cheese, meat, flour, juice, jam, vinegar, breads and wine.

One Dish Wonders: family style dining

featuring

simmering beef

2 pounds (.91 kg) shoulder roast, cubed
1/2 cup (125 mL) flour for dredging
2 tablespoons (30 mL) Ontario canola oil
12 pearl onions, peeled
2 garlic cloves, crushed
1 cup (250 mL) dry white wine
1/2 cup (125 mL) chicken stock
1 15-ounce can Ontario diced plum tomatoes
1 cup (250 mL) button mushrooms, quartered
1/2 teaspoon (2.5 mL) dried tarragon
1/2 teaspoon (2.5 mL) dried thyme
1 bay leaf
Ontario salt

Put the flour in a plastic bag and season well with salt. Put cubes of beef in the bag a few at a time and shake the bag to completely coat each piece of beef. In a large skillet or casserole dish sauté the beef in half of the oil until browned on all sides. Remove from the skillet. Sauté the onions and garlic in the rest of the oil until tender. Add the wine and the stock and bring it to a boil. Return the meat to the skillet along with the tomatoes and mushrooms. Season with the salt, tarragon, thyme and bay leaf. Cover and cook on low heat until tender, about 1 hour and 15 minutes. Serves 4 to 6 people.

Ottawa

O'BRIEN FARMS
On-line sales and farmers' market availability

Dan O'Brien is a 4th generation cattle farmer. O'Brien's 200 Simmental cattle are age and lineage verified. At all times, O'Brien has cattle of different ages so he can offer a consistent supply of locally-raised, hormone-free beef. Simmental cattle are one of the oldest cattle breeds producing well marbled, rich tasting meat. O'Brien sells to chefs in the area from small butcher shops like The Piggy Market in Ottawa's Westboro Village to grand hotels such as the Chateau Laurier. You can find O'Brien at the Ottawa Farmers' Market at Lansdown Park and the Kanata Farmers' Market. www.obrienfarms.ca

13214 Morewood Road, Wincester

Essex County

VIDMAR ORGANIC FUNGI
Open daily 9 to 2 or by appointment, 519-736-8080

You say Portobello, the Vidmar's say Portobella, but no one can argue that Vidmar mushrooms are the freshest and best tasting. Zlatko Vidmar is often referred to as a "mushroom genius" by his son Denis. Zlatko spent his life learning everything there is to know about mushrooms in China, Vietnam and now in Amherstburg. The 30,000-square foot organic mushroom facility grows Cremini, Brown, Baby Portobella and Portobella mushrooms. At the Amherstburg Farmers' Market you're guaranteed the mushrooms are only hours old and if you buy from the mushroom farm, Denis recommends you go after 11 am so the mushrooms you buy are picked that morning. www.vidmar-fung.com

1175 2nd Concession Road N, Amherstburg

mushroom bread pudding

1 teaspoon (5 mL) country fresh butter
4 strips artisan bacon, diced
1/2 cup (125 mL) onion, diced
1 garlic clove, minced
8 ounces (200 g) button mushrooms, chopped
1/2 teaspoon (2.5 mL) fresh thyme leaves, chopped
5 cups (1.25 L) day-old artisan bread,
cubed into 1-inch pieces
2 cups (500 mL) whipping cream
1 cup (250 mL) whole milk
6 farm fresh eggs, beaten
3/4 cup (180 mL) grated parmesan cheese
Ontario salt

Preheat the oven to 350F (180C). Grease a casserole dish with the butter and set aside.

Place a skillet over medium heat and cook the bacon. Cook, stirring often, until the bacon is browned and crispy, about 8 minutes. Remove the bacon. Add the onions and sauté until translucent, about 3 to 4 minutes. Add the garlic, mushrooms and thyme and cook until the mushrooms have released their water, about 10 minutes. Season the mushrooms with salt. Remove the pan from the heat and transfer the mushrooms to a large bowl. Allow them to cool completely and then add the bread.

In a separate bowl, whisk together the cream, milk, and eggs and 1/2 cup of the cheese. Season and pour the egg mixture over the bread and mushrooms. Fold in the crispy bacon and allow mixture to sit for at least 30 minutes or overnight. Once the bread has absorbed most of the custard, pour it into the casserole dish and sprinkle the top with the remaining cheese. Bake until golden brown and set in the centre, about 40 to 45 minutes. Serves 6.

enjoy with

KAWARTHA COUNTRY WINERY
Baco Noir
www.kawarthacountrywines.ca

cranberry beef stew

2 tablespoons (30 mL) Ontario soy oil
2 tablespoons (30 mL) country fresh butter
2 pounds (.91 kg) stewing beef or lamb
2 garlic cloves, minced
1 onion, diced
3/4 cup (180 mL) Muskoka Lakes cranberry wine
3/4 cup (180 mL) beef broth
2 tablespoons (30 mL) red wine vinegar
1 tablespoon (15 mL) tomato paste
1 1/2 cups (375 mL) fresh cranberries
1/3 cup (80 mL) light brown sugar, packed
2 tablespoons (30 mL) all-purpose flour
Ontario salt

Heat half the oil and butter in a 6-quart oven-proof pot over medium heat. Add half the meat, season well and brown on all sides. Remove the meat and repeat with remaining oil, butter and meat. Remove the second batch of meat from the pot. Add garlic and onions and cook until soft. Return the meat to the pot and add wine, broth, vinegar and tomato paste. Bring to a boil and immediately reduce to simmer. Cover and cook until meat is tender, about 2 hours. Chop half the cranberries with brown sugar and flour. Add chopped and whole cranberries to the pot, stir and cook for an additional 20 minutes. Season well and serve warm. Serves 4 to 6.

> A glass of fine VQA wine with a meal made from locally grown ingredients and you have a recipe for pure Zen-like bliss.
>
> Donald Ziraldo

Muskoka

JOHNSTON'S CRANBERRY MARSH
Open daily, year round from 9 to 5, Sunday 11 to 4

Cranberries don't grow in water, but they are flooded during harvest to make picking easier. Wendy Hogarth and Murray Johnston grow 27 acres of delicious cranberries on their beautiful 350-acre farm in the rugged Muskoka region. They offer tours, trails and an on-farm market featuring everything cranberry from preserves and baked goods to dried cranberries and even wine. Muskoka Lakes Winery produces a variety of excellent cranberry wines that are available through the LCBO.
www.savourmuskoka.com | www.cranberry.ca

1074 Cranberry Road, Bala

sourdough sausage quiche

enjoy with

CLOSSON CHASE VINEYARDS
Chardonnay
www.clossonchase.com

1 round artisan sourdough loaf
2 field zucchini, sliced
1 hot Italian-style sausage link
6 farm fresh eggs, beaten
1/2 cup (125 mL) whipping cream
3 ounces (75 g) Ontario chevre cheese
1/4 cup (60 mL) Ontario parmesan cheese
Ontario salt

Slice the top off the sourdough loaf and remove the bread in the centre, leaving a shell. Set aside.

Preheat the oven to 350F (180C). Slice the zucchini, season and cook for 10 minutes in a single layer on a baking sheet. Remove from oven, turn them over and bake an additional 10 minutes. Remove and set aside to cool. Meanwhile, remove the sausage meat from the casing and cook in a skillet until crispy.

In a separate bowl, mix the eggs and cream and season well. Slice the goat cheese log. Place the sourdough shell on a baking tray lined with parchment paper. Fill the sourdough with layers of zucchini, sausage meat and chevre, finishing off with sausage. Top with parmesan. Bake for 1 hour, 10 minutes, then leave to cool before slicing. Makes 1 loaf.

If you've eaten today,
thank a farmer.

Thunder Bay

THUNDER OAK CHEESE
On site retail shop open Monday to Saturday, 9 to 5

Both Jacob and Margaret Schep are from cheese-making families in Holland. Here in Ontario they make gouda cheese from their own herd of Holstein cows. The Scheps control the quality of milk and cheese making so you can be guaranteed the highest quality. Thunder Oak Cheese gouda won the Grand Prix award from the Dairy Farmers of Canada. www.cheesefarm.ca

755 Boundary Drive West, Neebing

local food in

Lanark County

Lanark County boasts outdoor adventure and quaint historic villages where local food is a form of expression, where maple syrup pours from every table and the garlic growers are award winners.

MAPLE SYRUP CAPITAL

The maple syrup capital of Ontario, Lanark County has more pancake houses and sugar camp restaurants than any other county. Some sugar camps are more formal with a greater choice of dishes on the menu. But whether a pancake house or sugar camp, the secret pancake recipes have been handed down for generations, for the lightest, fluffiest pancakes you'll ever experience. For some sweet fun you'll want to take in the Festival of the Maples in April and add a visit to the Maple Museum.

QUAINT LITTLE TOWNS

This region is blessed with so many small towns and villages so close together that you can hike or bike your way from one to the other. Perth is the main town of this region and it boasts more than 100 preserved stone heritage properties, some built by the very Scottish stonemasons who built the Rideau Canal. Both TV Ontario and Harrowsmith Country Magazine have awarded Perth the title of the 'Prettiest Town in Ontario'.

Quaint little towns like Carleton Place and Maberly boast chefs who are committed to locally produced food. At Ballygiblins Restaurant,

try their hamburgers made with Alpenblick Farm meat and their own house-made condiments. Jon and I also recommend Paul and Michele Zammit of Fall River Pub and Grill in Maberly, who offer pure meats and produce from local suppliers.

LAND OF GARLIC

Lanark County may not be the largest producer of garlic in the province, but they seem to love it more than any other. Their Garlic Festival, held every August, was rated the 5th best garlic festival in the world! Here you'll find (among other delicacies) garlic fudge and garlic ice cream.

Just outside Maberly is Beaver Pond Estates, a destination for all serious garlic lovers. Paul and Mary Lou Pospisil tend their research plot with more than 150 different varieties of garlic; offer garlic workshops and lots and lots of garlic advice. If you'd like to grow your own garlic, the Pospisil's will sell you seed garlic too.

CULINARY ENTREPRENEURS

The regional bounty inspires many culinary entrepreneurs like Caroline Ouellette of Ouellette Farm in Middleville. In their on-farm market you'll find delicious products such as grapeseed oil from a Niagara producer and local blueberry balsamic vinegar – yum!

Lanark County has a local food web directory, agriculture and culinary map, 7 farmers' markets and lots of markets on farms that offer fresh food in season.

Local Flavour
www.lanarklocalflavour.ca

Norfolk County

BERLO'S BEST SWEET POTATOES
Wholesale with some retail on farm. Call for availability 519-426-1500

Sherry VanBerlo and family grow 800 acres of sweet potatoes producing almost 15 million pounds a year. They are the largest sweet potato producer in Canada. There are no on-farm sales, but look for them in your grocery store. Ontario sweet potatoes have eyes and the skin is not smooth and glossy. You don't even have to peel the skin from a Berlo sweet potato because they're grown as naturally as possible and they're safe to eat. Chances are if you find "Ontario" sweet potatoes, they're Berlo's Best. www.berlosbest.com

325 Concession 13 Townsend Road, Simcoe

farmer's pie

2 Ontario sweet potatoes
2 tablespoons (30 mL) Ontario canola oil
1 medium onion, chopped
1 clove garlic, chopped
3/4 cup (175 mL) chopped mixed vegetables such as carrots, peas, peppers, corn or anything else you have in the refrigerator
1 1/2 pounds (.65 kg) lean ground beef
2 tablespoons (30 mL) all-purpose flour
1/4 cup (60 mL) Ontario whisky (optional)
1 beef bouillon cube
6 fresh thyme sprigs, leaves removed
1/2 cup (125 mL) Ontario white cheddar cheese, grated
1 tablespoon (15 mL) country fresh butter
2 tablespoons (30 mL) whole milk
1 green onion, sliced
Ontario salt

Preheat oven to 375F (190C). Peel sweet potatoes. Cut into chunks and put in a pan covered with salted water. Bring to a boil, reduce heat to a simmer and cook sweet potatoes until done, about 20 minutes. Drain and allow to steam dry.

Meanwhile, in a large skillet, heat oil over medium heat. Cook onion and garlic for 1 minute or until onions are soft. Add the vegetables and cook for 5 minutes. Add the ground beef and cook until no longer pink, about 8 to 10 minutes. Sprinkle flour over meat and mix well. Add whisky (use water if preferred), bouillon, thyme and season well. Cook stirring for 2 to 3 minutes or until flavours are well incorporated.

Spoon meat mixture into a 5 cup (1.25 L) casserole dish and top with half the cheddar. Set aside. Mash sweet potatoes with butter and milk. Season well. Spoon mixture over beef and top with remaining cheese and green onions. Bake for 30 minutes or until bubbly. Let stand for 5 minutes. Serves 4 to 6.

enjoy with

ROSEWOOD ESTATE
Merlot
www.rosewoodwine.com

enjoy with

13TH STREET WINERY
Cabernet Franc
www.13thstreetwinery.com

winter wine roast

2 pounds (.90 kg) pork short ribs, cut into 2-rib pieces
all-purpose flour for dredging
1 tablespoon (15 mL) Ontario canola oil
1 pound (.45 kg) Italian-style sausage,
cut into 3-inch pieces
1 onion, peeled and quartered
1 cup (250 mL) dry Ontario red wine
1/2 cup (125 mL) tomato paste
1 cup (250 mL) beef broth
2 garlic cloves, sliced
4 carrots, peeled and chopped
6 potatoes, peeled and diced
3 turnips, peeled and diced
1/2 small head cabbage, quartered
Ontario salt
loaf of country style artisan bread

Preheat oven to 350F (180C). Dust the short ribs with a bit of flour and brown in a large ovenproof skillet with canola oil. Remove from pan and add the sausage. Brown on all sides. Return the ribs to the skillet and add the onion.

In a bowl, mix the wine, tomato paste, broth and garlic, season well. Stir to combine and pour over meat in the skillet. Cover and transfer to the oven, roast slowly for 3 hours.

Remove from the oven and add the carrots, potatoes, turnips and cabbage. Add water if the sauce becomes too thick. Roast for an additional hour. When the potatoes are cooked through, remove from the oven and let it rest for about 15 minutes before serving. Serve with plenty of country-style artisan bread. Serves 4 to 6.

Toronto

ONTARIO NATURAL FOOD CO-OP
Order desk open Monday through Friday from 9 to 4:30

They began with natural and organic foods and they're moving into local foods. One of Ontario's largest packaged food co-ops has 13 local food products that include crushed, diced and whole organic Ontario tomatoes (canned with no BSP), firm and extra firm organic tofu and a variety of herbs all grown in Ontario. The line is called From Seed to Plate. www.onfc.ca

5685 McLaghlin Road, Mississauga

enjoy with
EASTDELL ESTATES WINERY
Black Cab
www.eastdell.com

chunky chili

3 tablespoons (45 mL) canola oil
2 large onions, chopped
1 green bell pepper, chopped
1 red bell pepper, chopped
3 garlic cloves, minced
1 pound (454 grams) ground Ontario chicken
2 pounds (900 grams) Ontario pork butt,
cut into 1-inch (2.5 cm) cubes
1 28-ounce (680 grams) can diced Ontario tomatoes
1 tablespoon (15 mL) chili powder
1 or 2 large jalapeño chilies, seeded and minced
2 tablespoons (30 mL) ground cumin
1 16-ounce (386 grams) can red kidney beans, drained
1/2 cup (125 mL) Ontario dry red wine
Ontario salt

Heat oil in large pot over medium-high heat. Add onions, bell peppers and garlic and sauté until tender, about 10 minutes. Spoon mixture to a plate and add chicken and pork pieces to the pot. Cook over medium-high heat until pork is no longer pink, stirring occasionally, about 10 minutes. Return onion mixture to the pot and add tomatoes (with liquid), chili powder, jalapeños and cumin. Season well. Cover the pot and simmer for about 1 hour, stirring occasionally. Remove the lid and add red kidney beans and red wine to the chili. Simmer, uncovered until chili thickens, about 30 minutes. Adjust seasoning. Ladle into bowls. Serves 6.

Prescott & Russell

MARIPOSA FARM
Open for Sunday Brunch only

Ian Walker is a vocal and flamboyant restaurant farmer. He and partner Suzanne Lavoie raise heritage breeds of pigs, geese and duck. Ian also grows heritage tomatoes, beets and carrots. All of this produce and more he collects from other local farmers is distributed to over 160 restaurants throughout Ottawa. The on-farm restaurant serves dishes of food from Mariposa Farm and its local suppliers. Each dish is prepared and displayed on the wooden counter (Ian himself crafted) as an irresistible living menu of the day's offerings. www.mariposa-ducks.on.ca

6468 County Road 17, Plantagenet

People who pull carrots from the earth or sift through sacks of potatoes with soil still clinging to them will make the connection between their food and the place it comes from.

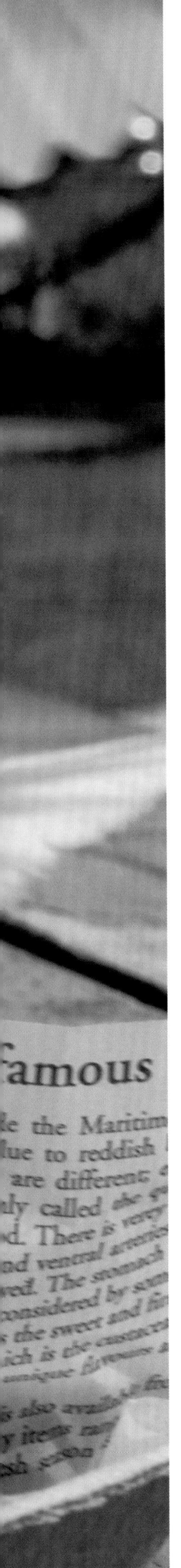

Great Lakes Fish

featuring

enjoy with

LAILEY VINEYARD
Chardonnay
www.laileyvineyard.com

brown butter pickerel

1 medium head cauliflower, chopped
1 cup (250 mL) whole milk
3 cups (750 mL) chicken stock
2 tablespoons (30 mL) country fresh butter
4 pickerel fillets
1 tablespoon (15 mL) Ontario soy oil
6 tablespoons (90 mL) country fresh butter
1 garlic clove, minced
1/4 cup (60 mL) just-picked oregano leaves
1 tablespoon (15 mL) Ontario balsamic vinegar
Ontario salt

Place the cauliflower, milk and stock in a saucepan over high heat and bring to a boil. Reduce the heat to low, cover and cook for 20 minutes or until tender. Drain the cauliflower, reserving 2 tablespoons of the liquid. Place the cauliflower and liquid in the bowl of a food processor with the butter. Season and process until smooth. Set aside and keep warm.

Season the fish on both sides. Heat oil in a non-stick skillet over medium-high heat and cook the pickerel, skin side down for 4 to 5 minutes or until golden and crisp. Turn over and cook for a further 3 to 4 minutes or until cooked through. Remove from the pan and keep pickerel warm. Add the butter, garlic and oregano and cook for 1 minute or until browned. Remove from heat and stir through the vinegar. Top the purée with the fish and spoon over the oregano butter. Serves 4.

Niagara

MINOR FISH
Open year round with winter and summer hours

Minor Fish is a business owned and operated by the Minor family in Port Colborne. They fish the waters of Lake Erie and in their little fish shack they sell fresh, frozen and smoked pickerel, perch, smelt and whitefish. I recommend the fantastic fish (perch) and chip order (only $4.50 and ooh so good!). Stand in line from the take-out window and sit at one of the bistro tables on the sidewalk and eat canalside, or go inside for the full bustling experience.

176 West Street, Port Colborne

local food in the

Holland Marsh

You see it, but perhaps you just don't understand what it is: the word "Bradford" on bags of carrots, onions or beets. These staple vegetables come from the Holland Marsh, and while they may just be carrots, onions or beets to you, to the Holland Marsh growers, they're 'gold'.

This small, 12,000-acre pocket of the most fertile soil in the country, is known as Ontario's soup and salad bowl. I guarantee you've never seen so many onions, carrots, lettuce and celery during harvest as you will in the Holland Marsh. And because the vegetables are grown, stored, processed and packaged in the Holland Marsh, the entire distribution chain is shortened, reducing our food miles exponentially.

RIVERS & DYKES

If you're wondering how only 64 farmers can grow such a wealth of vegetables in a wet marshland, know that it's because they've developed and constructed a complex canal system with dykes (some 28-kilometres long) that divert the water from the Holland River. Today it's not so much a wetland, as it is a charming agricultural community with canals, straight-line trenches and dykes that contrast the jet black soil with the brilliant green of the vegetables. It is definitely Ontario's most visually vibrant agricultural region. For me, standing on Canal Road and gazing at the endless checkerboard fields of sprouting plants on rich soil so vibrantly black inspires me to want to run out there and plant something – and you will too.

The Holland Marsh has a local food web directory, agriculture and culinary map, farmers' markets and lots of markets on farms that offer fresh food in season.

Holland Marsh Gold
www.hollandmarshgold.com

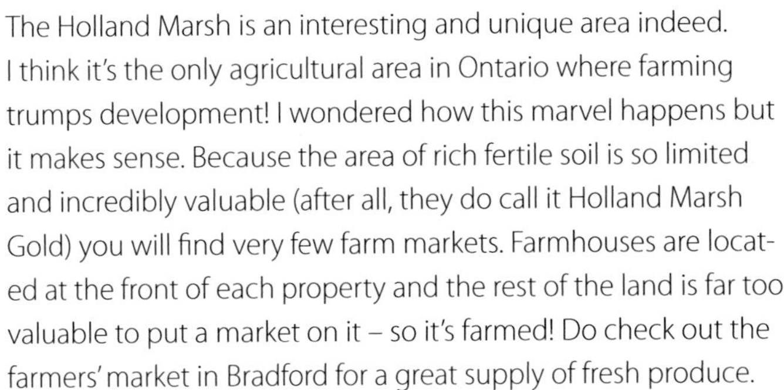

The Holland Marsh is an interesting and unique area indeed. I think it's the only agricultural area in Ontario where farming trumps development! I wondered how this marvel happens but it makes sense. Because the area of rich fertile soil is so limited and incredibly valuable (after all, they do call it Holland Marsh Gold) you will find very few farm markets. Farmhouses are located at the front of each property and the rest of the land is far too valuable to put a market on it – so it's farmed! Do check out the farmers' market in Bradford for a great supply of fresh produce.

YOU CAN TASTE THE DIFFERENCE

I'm so happy to be eating Holland Marsh produce 12 months of the year. They grow everything from salad lettuces and seasonal vegetables that carry us through the spring and summer, to a full range of root vegetables that carry us through the fall and winter. I love their potatoes; they're larger than most with a high water content and less starch, making them great for frying and mashing. In fact, I can't leave the Holland Marsh without my arms laden with exciting produce – sweet corn and shallots, multi-coloured carrots and candy cane beets. Oh my gosh, I'm getting excited all over again.

PICK A FESTIVAL

The best time to visit the Holland Marsh is during one of their festivals. Soup Fest takes place in October and Carrot Fest is in August, both in Bradford; and Feast of Fields in September. If you can't make it out there, chances are you can catch the Holland Marsh growers on TV. The Fresh Life is a show pairing chefs with Holland Marsh farmers. It runs on both Rogers TV and Sun TV.

enjoy with
THE GRANGE TRUMPOUR'S
Mill Chardonnay
www.grangeofprinceedward.com

chardonnay buttered yellow perch

4 yellow perch fillets
2 tablespoons (30 mL) country fresh butter
2 garlic cloves, minced
1/2 cup (125 mL) chardonnay or dry white Ontario wine
1 teaspoon (5 mL) field parsley, minced
2 tablespoons (30 mL) country fresh butter
Ontario salt

Season the perch. Melt the butter in a skillet and sauté the garlic for 2 minutes on medium heat. Add the wine and bring liquid to a boil. Reduce by half. Add the perch and cook until fish is cooked through, about 5 minutes. Sprinkle with parsley and cook for another minute. Remove perch to a warm platter and add butter to the skillet juices. Cook over medium heat, stirring as the butter melts. Cook for another minute or until sauce is glossy. Serve warm perch drizzled with chardonnay butter. Serves 4.

Norfolk County

PLEASANT PORT DISTRIBUTION
Open year round

George Gibbons is a second generation farmer, fishing the waters of Lake Erie for a daily catch of Ontario's famous Lake Erie Perch, Yellow Pickerel, Whitefish and Silver Bass. George's day begins on the water at daybreak and on a good day he's back anywhere from noon to 6 or 7 pm. Fishing season is from March to October. "It's always best when it's fresh," says George, who sells to area restaurants. You can find Quinn, third generation Gibbons, selling fresh fish at the Silver Lake Farmers' Market in Port Dover; frozen fish in the winter.

Port Dover & Lake Erie

Oxford County

OAK MANOR
On-farm shop open 6 days a week, closed Sunday

Recognized by the Organic Trade Association as a leader in organic agriculture, Dave Riebling stone grinds 12 different organic flours from all-purpose to spelt and rye; a dozen cereals from quick-cooking oats to 7-grain cereals and other products such as flax seeds, pearl barley and popcorn. He sources everything he can from local organic farms and to make sure the farms follow common organic principles, Dave developed the first in-house verification program to guarantee the organic nature of the farms he buys from. www.oakmanorfarms.com

756907 Oxford County Road #5, Tavistock

pickerel cheeks with bacon and crispy sage

4 strips artisan bacon, roughly chopped
1 cup (250 mL) Ontario cornmeal
1 teaspoon (5 mL) cayenne pepper
canola oil for frying
16 sage leaves
1 pound (.45 g) pickerel cheeks
Ontario salt

Cook the bacon in a large skillet until crispy. Remove from heat. Meanwhile, mix the cornmeal with the cayenne and season well. Heat a deep pot with about 2 inches of oil over medium-high heat. Drop the sage leaves into the oil a few at a time. Cook for approximately 30 seconds and remove with a slotted spoon. Drain on paper towels.

Season the pickerel cheeks well, then dredge in the cornmeal. Shake off any excess and fry in the oil. Cook in batches if you need to but don't overcrowd in the pot. Cook for approximately 3 to 4 minutes. Put the cooked cheeks in the skillet with the bacon. Continue until all cheeks are cooked. Toss cheeks with bacon allowing the juices to flavour the cheeks. Serve garnished with crispy sage leaves. Serves 4 to 6.

potted lake trout

1 1/2 cups (375 mL) lake trout
3/4 cup (180 mL) farm fresh butter, cut into cubes
2 spring onions, sliced
3 tablespoons (45 mL) Niagara verjus
pinch of paprika
handful of dill
Ontario salt

Preheat oven to 350F (180C). Season trout with salt and bake on a rack in a roasting pan for 30 minutes or until cooked through. Remove from oven and set aside to cool.

Melt the butter in a small pan and set aside. In a bowl break up the trout into small pieces and mix with onions, verjus, paprika and the dill. Season, then divide between 4 little pots or 1 large one. Top with the melted butter and chill for a few hours. Serve with bread or crostini. Serves 4 to 6.

Grey Bruce County

AKIWENZIE'S FISH
Factory store open Monday to Friday, 9 to 5

Andrew Akiwenzie is a lover of the water, especially the waters of Georgian Bay. He leaves early in the morning and returns each day with a catch of whitefish and lake trout. On good days, he finds rainbow trout and salmon in his nets. Andrew fishes until the ice forms on the water and begins again when the ice melts; in a mild year, he fishes continually. Andrew's wife Natasha cleans, bones and smokes the fish in a variety of flavours including regular, honey garlic, tandoori and Cajun. You can find Andrew and his children at the Brickworks Farmers' Market, Green Barns (Wychwood) and the Orangeville Farmers' Market.

171 Lakeshore Boulevard, Wiarton

enjoy with
Rosehall Run
Sullyzwicker Rose
www.rosehallrun.com

rainbow trout tacos

1/2 cup (125 mL) all-purpose flour
1/2 teaspoon (2.5 mL) baking powder
1/2 teaspoon (2.5 mL) salt
1/2 cup (125 mL) Ontario beer
6 tablespoons (90 mL) mayonnaise
4 tablespoons (60 mL) sour cream
Ontario vegetable oil for deep frying
8 flour tortillas
2 Ontario rainbow trout fillets
1/4 small white cabbage, very thinly sliced
1 small tomato, diced
Niagara verjus
fresh garden coriander sprigs

Sift the flour, baking powder and salt into a bowl. Gradually whisk in beer to make a smooth batter. Cover and set aside for 30 minutes. Mix the mayo and sour cream and set aside.

Preheat oven to 300F (150C). Wrap the tortillas in foil and warm through in the oven.

Heat the oil in a large saucepan. Remove the skin from the fillets by running a sharp knife along the bottom of the fillet in between the skin and the flesh. Season the fillets and cut each into 1-inch wide strips. Using tongs, dunk a few pieces in the batter. One at a time, drop 4 pieces into the hot oil. Deep fry for 3 minutes until crisp and golden. Remove with a slotted spoon and drain on paper towels. Add 4 more pieces to the oil, and repeat until all pieces of fish are fried.

To assemble, spread some mayo mixture down the centre of a warmed tortilla and scatter over a little cabbage. Place deep rainbow trout pieces down the centre and spoon over some diced tomatoes. Drizzle with a little verjus. Top with coriander, roll up and serve. Repeat for each of the tacos.

Note: the stronger the beer, the better the flavour. However, even a light ale will work.

Waterloo County

LYNDON FISH HATCHERIES
Open Good Friday to Thanksgiving weekend, daily from 8 to 5

In 2000, Lynn Rieck and partner Sean Pressey started a fish hatcherie selling fingerling rainbow trout to the wholesale market. For consumers, they created a 1.5 acre, natural spring pond that is always stocked with thousands of feisty rainbow trout. If you're not into fishing, you can certainly buy fresh, frozen trout fillets as well as smoked. Lyndon has a second location on Manitoulin Island and they once raised beautiful Arctic Char before low-priced imports made it impossible to continue - pity. www.lyndonfishhatcheries.com

1745 Huron Road, Petersburg

Drive through rural Ontario and discover the delicious places you never knew existed.

local food in

Ottawa

I'm so proud of our nation's capital. With a population of 850,000, there are an unbelievable1,276 farms inside the city limits! This is an urban space that feeds itself!

GASTRO ALLEY

For a decadent flavour of the region, go to Murray Street, or as the locals call it, 'gastro-alley'. Here there are five chef-owned restaurants – Navarra, Murray Street Cafe, Sweetgrass Aboriginal Bistro, Domas Restaurant and Benny's Bistro – that all promote local dishes, each in their own unrivaled way.

FARMERS' MARKETS

Just around the corner from gastro-alley is the Byward Farmers' Market. It's a huge market that occupies a few streets. Along Byward Street you'll find small artisan shops like the House of Cheese. This tiny shop is overloaded with cheeses from Ontario and Quebec. Interestingly, many of the Quebec cheeses are considered local because they're produced within the 100-mile radius that most deem necessary to make this claim.

On York Street is Aubrey's Meat Market. Owner Brian Henley works with local meats exclusively. Recently, he had an idea to get more people into his shop, so he sold coupons worth $175 for produce in his shop for only $55! Within a few days, he had sold well over 3,000 coupons. The day I was there, most of his shelves were empty with eager customers cashing in. But Henley had sold more than meat and produce; most of them were new customers interested in the concept of eating local.

Saturday mornings are the liveliest time at the market, with stalls overflowing with fresh produce ranging from market vegetables in the summer to root vegetables, maple syrup and honey in the winter. BeaverTails are delicious fried disks of whole wheat dough, shaped like a beaver tail and topped with all things sweet – yum!

The Ottawa Farmers' Market, in Lansdowne Park, is a true locavore farmers' market with meat producers, organic vegetable producers and more. Artisan bread bakers offer seductive loaves and specialty goods like gluten-free products. It's here that Dave Neil got his start in the charcuterie business. Dave started with a stand at the market, built up a clientele, and then opened his shop, The Piggy Market (www.

thepiggymarket.com) on Winston Avenue. Indeed, farmers' markets serve as incubators for many new businesses. Another is Pascale's Ice Cream (www.pascalesicecream.com). Pascale Berthiaue's all natural ice cream flavours are inspired by the fresh produce that surrounds her at the market.

NATIONAL ARTS CENTRE

Le Café is The National Art Centre's restaurant, run by one of the province's unbeatable chefs, Michael Blackie. Blackie promotes local food enthusiastically throughout his menus and told me, "These days, a chef cannot afford not to be using local food in his kitchen." During watermelon season, Blackie made a dish of compressed watermelon and rack of lamb – it was amazing! And I am totally committed to his mushroom macchiatto. It's his version of cream of mushroom bisque and I guarantee it will be one of your most memorable flavour experiences – ever! The mushrooms come from Le Coprin Mushroom Farm.

ACCOMMODATION

If you're spending the night in Ottawa, choose The Arc Hotel. Executive Chef Jason Duffy's menus read like a geography lesson on the area's farms and you can get a true taste of the region through his cooking.

Of course, an overnight stay at the Chateau Laurier is the stuff of dreams. It's also home to an event called Savour Ottawa; a farmer tradeshow eagerly attended by chefs in the capital city. In each booth farmers display photos of their summer produce and samples of their year round products. They talk with chefs that rush in and out all day long – about produce, prices and delivery. It's an event that fills more Ottawa restaurants with more local food.

> Ottawa has a local food web directory, agriculture and culinary map, 7 farmers' markets and lots of markets on farms that offer fresh food in season.
>
> Buy Local Food Guide | www.justfood.ca

enjoy with
CALAMUS ESTATE WINERY
Barrel Aged Chardonnay
www.calamuswines.com

salmon cakes

1 pound (.45 kg) fresh salmon, cooked
2 white flesh potatoes, mashed
2 tablespoons (30 mL) country fresh butter, melted
1 tablespoon (15 mL) whole grain mustard
1 teaspoon (5 mL) fresh dill, chopped
1 teaspoon (5 mL) fresh parsley, chopped
1/2 cup (125 mL) breadcrumbs
3 tablespoons (45 mL) Ontario canola oil
Ontario salt

Break up the salmon into small pieces. Put it in a bowl with mashed potato, melted butter, mustard, fresh dill and parsley. Season with salt and mix thoroughly. Divide the mixture into 8 equal portions and roll each into a ball shape before flattening them to make patties. Dredge the fish cake patties with bread crumbs, making sure they are evenly coated.

Heat the oil in the frying pan until it is very hot, then fry the fish cakes in batches of 2 until each one is crisp and golden. Makes 8 salmon cakes.

Ottawa

GRENVILLE HERB FARM
Farmers' markets sales

Bill Langenberg grows large flats of fresh garden herbs for the hospitality industry and smaller containers for his farm market sales. A retired horticulture professor at Kemptville College, Bill grows herbs using only organic seed and organic production practices in a temperature-controlled greenhouse. While Bill is hesitant to make any health claims for herbs, he does state that herbs have high antioxidant levels and growing them organically intensifies the phenolic compounds. You can find Bill's fresh herbs at the North Gower, Kemptville and Merrickville Farmers' Markets from May to October. www.savourottawa.ca

2860 Donnelly Drive, Ottawa

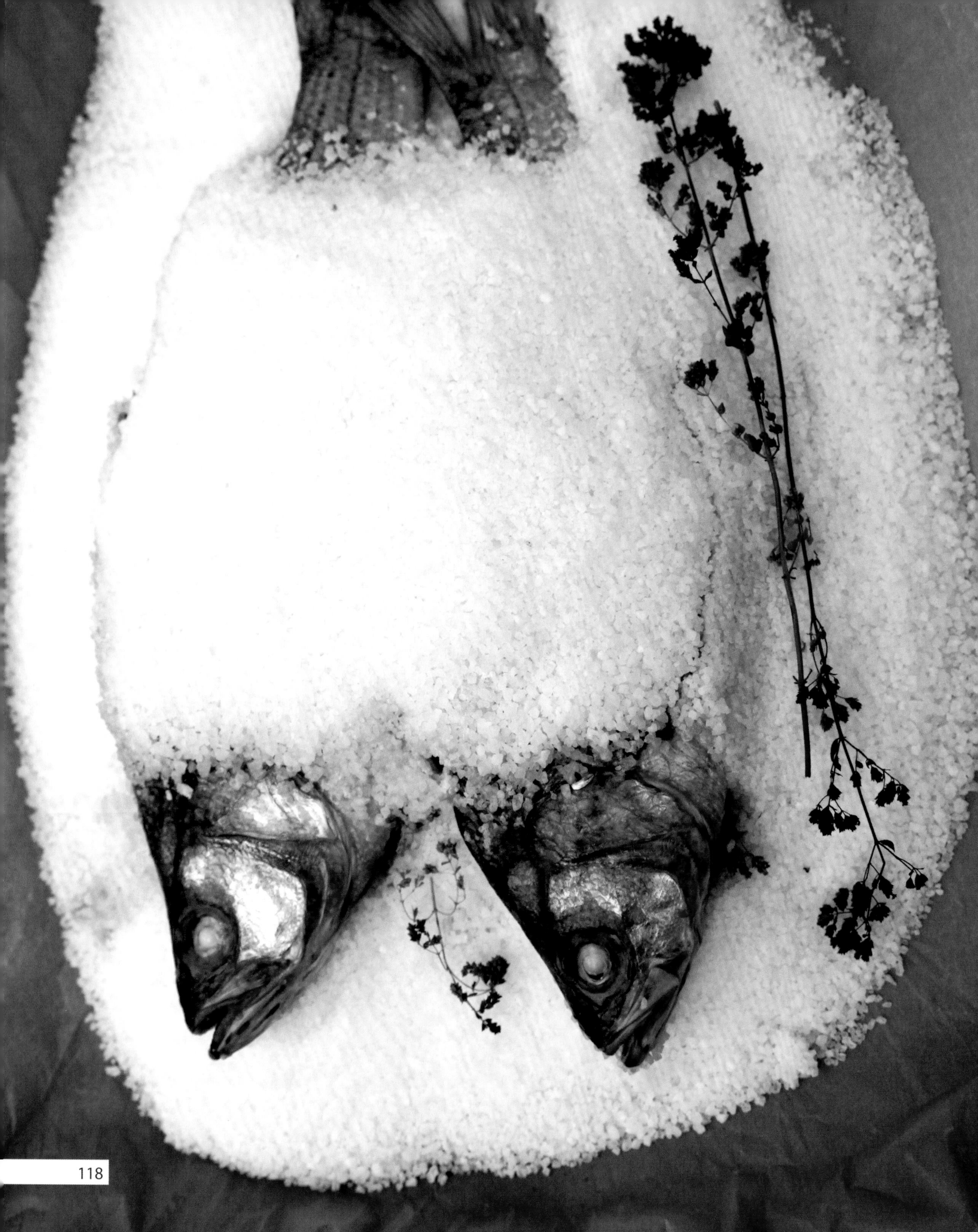

salt crusted silver bass

2 whole silver bass, approx 1.5 pounds each
8 parsley sprigs
4 tablespoons (60 mL) Niagara verjus
2 kg box coarse Ontario salt
4 sprigs dried oregano
Ontario salt

Preheat oven to 425F (220C). Stuff the cavity of the bass with parsley, season it and drizzle in the verjus. Lay about ½-inch bed of salt on the bottom of baking sheet which has been lined with parchment paper. Place the fish and dried oregano over the salt and cover the fish with the remaining salt. There should be a ½-inch salt crust on top of the fish as well. It is not necessary to cover the head and tail. Bake for 35 to 40 minutes. Remove from the oven. To serve, crack the salt crust tableside. Wipe all of the salt away from the fish and enjoy. Serves 4 to 6.

enjoy with

NIAGARA COLLEGE TEACHING WINERY
Dean's List Chardonnay
www.teachingwinery.ca

Huron County

SIFTO SALT
Available in most grocery stores

So valuable was salt to Huron County that it was used as money in the 1800s. Goderich is home to the largest rock salt mine in the world and the Sifto Salt Company. I don't know of anyone who doesn't remember the cylinder of Sifto Salt in the cupboard growing up. The 136-year old company mines over 8 million tonnes of Ontario salt a year from ancient sea beds 1,800 feet below the surface. Varieties include culinary, super-fine and kosher salt. Salt is indispensable in cooking and it's comforting to know that we can make a choice and buy local salt with the Sifto name. www.siftocanada.com

245 Regent Street, Goderich

smoked trout and chive tortilla

1 large field potato, diced
1 teaspoon (5 mL) country fresh butter
6 farm fresh eggs, beaten
small bunch garden chives, chopped
4 ounces (100g) smoked Ontario lake trout, skin removed and flaked
Ontario salt

Drop the potato into boiling salted water and cook for 8 to 10 minutes. Drain and leave in the pot to evaporate the remaining water.

Heat butter in a small non-stick oven-proof skillet over medium low heat. Whisk the eggs with potato chunks, half the chives and the trout. Pour into the pan and leave to sit for a minute. Cook, drawing in the sides to let the uncooked egg get to the edges. When the base is almost set, sprinkle with remaining chives and slide it under a hot broiler for a few minutes to finish cooking the top. Do not brown. Cut into wedges and serve. Serves 4 to 6.

Oxford County

GOOSSEN'S TROUT FARM
Open year round, call first.

It was once a tobacco farm but now Brian and Sue Goossen raise delicious fresh water trout. If you call ahead, you can buy them right from their charming 260-acre farm in Otterville either whole, cleaned or filleted. The drive is beautiful and when the succulent fillets are cooked, they have a fresh, clean character that is refreshingly addictive. Many restaurants in Oxford County serve Goossen's trout; just ask for it. Who knew trout could be so exciting? www.oxfordbuylocal.ca

165548 New Road, Otterville, 519-879-6352

Eating local means you help keep farmers in business and they help keep you fed. The sustainability of that exchange makes more sense to me than gambling on faceless producers thousands of miles from my home.

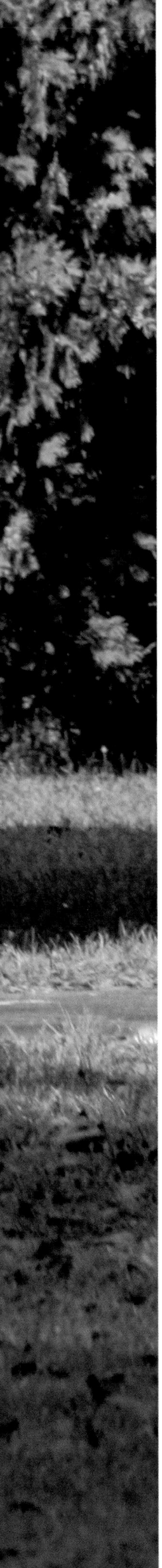

Farmyard Fowl

featuring

apple cider brined chicken

3 cups (750 mL) water
4 cups (1 L) Ontario apple cider
1/4 cup (60 mL) Ontario salt
1 tablespoon (15 mL) black peppercorns
3 bay leaves
1 (6-pound) roasting chicken, cut up into pieces
1 cup (250 mL) Ontario apple cider

Combine the water, cider, salt, peppercorns and bay leaves in a saucepan and bring to a boil. Stir until salt dissolves. Remove from heat and cool.

Meanwhile, clean the chicken and trim excess fat. Place chicken in a deep dish and cover with cooled brine. Add enough water to cover the chicken if necessary. Refrigerate 8 hours or overnight, making sure all pieces remain submerged in the brine.

Preheat oven to 375F (190C). Remove chicken from the brine and lay on a rack in a roasting pan. Bake for 55 minutes to an hour. Meanwhile, bring apple cider to a boil on the stovetop. Reduce heat to a simmer and reduce to approximately ¼ cup, about 10 minutes. About 15 minutes before chicken is done, begin basting with apple cider reduction every 5 minutes or so, being careful not to burn the chicken. Remove from oven. Serves 4 to 6.

Norfolk County

THE CIDER KEG
Open seasonally May to December

Cheryl Peck prides herself on growing the finest quality Norfolk apples and pressing them into sparkling and flavoured ciders with only country goodness added. Their retail barn sits among the hundreds of acres of orchard and the journey from orchard to your table is simply a drive to The Cider Keg. While you're there, be prepared to be tempted with fresh baked apple pie from their on-site bakery. www.ciderkeg.com

1231 Hwy 24 South, Vittoria

enjoy with
STRATUS
Sauvignon Blanc
www.stratuswines.com

LONG DOG WINERY
Pinot Noir
www.longdog.ca

blackberry duck

1 5- to 6-lb Ontario Muscovy duck
2 cups (500 mL) boilinghot water
1 tablespoon (15 mL) Ontario salt
1/2 cup (125 mL) ripe blackberries
2 tablespoons (30 mL) Ontario sparkling wine
1 teaspoon (5 mL) brown sugar
1 teaspoon (5 mL) country fresh butter
Ontario salt

Put oven rack in the middle of the oven and preheat oven to 425°F (220C). Remove and discard excess fat from body cavity and neck of duck, then rinse inside and out. Prick skin all over with a sharp fork. Place duck, breast side up, on a rack in a deep roasting pan. Slowly pour boiling hot water over duck to tighten the skin. Drain any water from cavity of the duck and pour out half the water from the pan. The water should not touch the bottom of the duck. Sprinkle the salt inside the duck. Roast duck, breast side up for 45 minutes.

Meanwhile, place blackberries, sparkling wine and brown sugar in a small saucepan and heat over medium high heat. Cook for 2 minutes, or untill the blackberries break up easily with a fork. Remove from heat and stir in butter until melted.

Turn duck over using two large forks and roast 45 minutes more. Turn duck breast side up again, tilting duck to drain any liquid from cavity into pan. Continue to roast duck until skin is brown and crisp, about 45 minutes more. Total roasting time is about 2 1/4 hours. Transfer duck to a cutting board and let stand 15 minutes before carving. Discard liquid in roasting pan. Serve carved duck with plenty of blackberry sauce. Serves 4 to 6.

Northumberland County

BURNHAM FAMILY FARM
Open daily from June 1 to December 23

Farmers Paul and Anne Burnham have a 400 acre farm between Port Hope and Cobourg on a convenient Highway 2 location. From their farm, they grow raspberries, sweet corn, peaches, beans, popping corn and more. In their on-farm market, they sell all of their produce as well as the best from neighbouring farms. The Burnhams are conscious of the importance of local food so they create signs that tell you where each fruit and vegetable is from and how many kilometres it travelled to get to their market. www.burnhamfamilyfarmmarket.ca

7760 County Road 2, Cobourg

local food in

Thunder Bay

Thunder Bay is cattle country and has its own brand of local beef, called Superior Beef. Superior Beef is an assurance that the animals were born and raised in Thunder Bay and it is divided into two brands. Grass-Fed Beef is raised on a hay and grass diet and Grain-Fed Beef is given barley for the last 100 to 120 days. You can find Superior (Thunder Bay) Beef at Tarrymore Farms in South Gillies, Maki's Juswanna Farm, Reidridge Farms and Bruce and Valve Forrest Farm in Thunder Bay.

There are many more meat producers in Thunder Bay. Sandy Acres specializes in Black Angus and Limousin beef and Rob Walsh of Northern Unique raises pigs and wild boar. Little Doo's Farm raises lamb, rabbit and Muscovy Duck and Boreal Edge Farm raises young grass-fed cattle less than 18 months old.

NORTHERN BEAUTY

The Slate River Valley is a stunningly beautiful area to explore and it's here you'll find Errindale Farms with their naturally-raised high quality pork and lamb and Blue Moon Ranch with their grass-fed lamb and beef and a wide range of garden vegetables. Also in the valley is Breukelman's Potato Farm, selling uniquely delicious potatoes from their farm and at the Thunder Bay Country Market.

The beautiful Boreal forest in Northern Ontario is the largest forest in the province, covering 50 million hectares of rich terrain. The surrounding agricultural land is intense in its ability to grow delicious and distinctive vegetables.

The savoury and earthy flavours of birch syrup are completely different from maple syrup.

ARTISAN FARMERS

Renate Nitsche runs her family farm, Nature's Choice. She grows a huge variety of garden vegetables and sells them at the Thunder Bay Country Market. A great baker, Renate also offers baked goods. The De Bruins grow tomatoes, cucumbers, herbs and a variety of fresh lettuces in their greenhouses from May through to November.

Just west of Thunder Bay is the potato farm called B & B Farms. The Burgsteden family grows 200 acres of white, red and yellow flesh varieties of potatoes. You can buy potatoes fresh or processed into peeled, cubed and fresh cut fries.

BIRCH SYRUP

More than 500 birch trees are tapped for Boreal Birch Syrup (www.birchsyrup.ca). It's a unique gourmet product made by Dave Challen and Beth Kuiper. The savoury and earthy flavours of birch syrup are completely different from maple syrup. While it's still sweet enough to pour over pancakes, many people will glaze salmon, add it to a roasted squash soup or use it as a baking ingredient for a unique flavour. Gourmands in Toronto can find birch syrup at Culinarium and in Ottawa – check out La Bottega at the Byward Farmers' Market.

Thunder Bay has a local food web directory and lots of markets on farms that offer fresh food in season.

Get Fresh in Thunder Bay | www.nwofood.ca

Toronto

BERETTA ORGANIC FARM
Open Monday through Friday, 8 to 4

Wow, 800 amazing acres just outside Toronto belong to the Beretta family. Mike and Cynthia and their three children. On the farm are pasture cattle, pigs, sheep, chickens and turkey. The Berettas grow their own animal feed and process their animals themselves meaning they control the high organic standards from start to finish. You can find Beretta Organic meats at Whole Foods, Longo's and many independent grocers as well as the Dufferin Grove Farmers' Market. Sign up for their free newsletter to receive monthly news on farm experiences, tours, demonstrations and even cooking classes! www.berettaorganics.com

80 Galaxy Boulevard, Unit 1-3, Etobicoke

chicken wrapped with mushrooms

2 tablespoons (30 mL) country fresh butter
1/2 cup (125 mL) onions, finely chopped
6 cups (1.5 L) sliced mushrooms, whatever variety you can find at the farmers' market
2 garlic cloves, minced
2 packages puff pastry, thawed. Each package has 2 blocks of pastry and you'll need all 4
4 chicken breasts, boneless and skinless
2 teaspoons (10 mL) fresh thyme, minced
1 farm fresh egg, beaten
2 teaspoons (10 mL) water
1 tablespoon (15 mL) finely chopped fresh parsley leaves
Ontario salt

Preheat the oven to 375F (190C) and line a baking sheet with parchment paper.

Melt the butter in a large skillet over medium heat. Add the onions and cook for 2 minutes or until wilted. Add the mushrooms and garlic and season well. Cook for 4 to 6 minutes or until softened. Remove from the heat and cool completely. On a lightly floured surface, unfold 1 sheet of puff pastry. Gently roll the pastry out to 2 1/2 times the size of the chicken breast. Repeat with remaining 3 sheets of puff pastry.

Season both sides of the chicken breasts with thyme, and salt. Place each chicken breast on one half of each pastry. Spoon 1/2 cup of the mushroom mixture on top of each chicken breast. Brush the edges of the pastry lightly with the egg wash and fold the other half of the pastry over the chicken, wrapping to secure all edges. Fold the edges of the pastry to make a 1/2-inch border and pinch the ends tightly to seal completely. Cut 3 small slits in the top of each pastry.

Place the pastries on the prepared baking sheet and brush each with the remaining egg wash. Bake for 30 to 35 minutes or until the pastry is golden and the chicken is cooked through. Serves 4.

enjoy with

NORM HARDIE WINERY
County Pinot Noir
www.normanhardie.com

enjoy with

OAK HEIGHTS WINERY
Sauvignon Blanc
www.oakheights.ca

garlic roasted game hens with crispy sage

2 garlic cloves, minced
1/2 teaspoon (2.5 mL) Ontario hot pepper flakes
6 garden picked sage leaves
3 tablespoons (45 mL) Ontario canola oil
2 game hens or very small chickens, halved
4 garlic heads
crispy sage leaves
Ontario red wine vinegar for drizzling
Ontario salt

Preheat oven to 400F (200 C). Combine the garlic, hot pepper flakes, sage leaves and oil. Season well. Set aside. Lay the hens on a baking sheet lined with parchment paper. Slice the top of each garlic head, exposing the cloves inside and place on baking sheet with the hens. Brush all with garlic oil.

Roast for 55 minutes, basting periodically or until game hens are cooked through and the garlic is tender. Top with crispy sage leaves and drizzle with red wine vinegar. Serves 4.

Crispy sage leaves: fill a small saucepan with 1-inch of oil and heat over high heat. When oil is hot, drop 3 to 4 sage leaves into the hot oil and cook for one minute. Remove with tongs and drain on paper towels.

99.9% of the chicken you find in grocery stores is local.

Perth County

AUGUST'S HARVEST
No farm sales.

The aromas when harvesting 4 acres of garlic will whet any gourmand's appetite. Warren Ham, owner of August's Harvest, specializes in original and extra savoury varieties of garlic and shallots. Before the garlic harvest, scapes are cut off and sold to large grocery chains. Garlic harvest is around late July and the Garlic Festival in September. A little-known fact is that Warren grows an additional 4-acres of vegetables that are harvested just for the food box programs in Toronto. Look for August's Harvest products in your favourite grocery store or buy on-line at www.augustsharvest.com, www.savourstratford.com

4727 Road 130, Gadshill

lemongrass chicken skewers

2 cloves garlic, minced
3 tablespoons (45 mL) Ontario canola oil
1/2 cup (125 mL) Ontario maple syrup
2 teaspoons (10 mL) Ontario soy sauce
1 teaspoon (5 mL) dry mustard
2 teaspoons (10 mL) Niagara verjus
4 boneless, skinless chicken breast halves
12 Niagara lemongrass stalks
Ontario salt

Put the garlic, oil, syrup, soy, mustard and verjus in a bowl. Season and whisk to combine. Pound each chicken breast to an even thickness. Cut each one lengthwise into 3 strips and let marinate in the maple syrup marinade for 3 or 4 hours in the refrigerator. Remove the outer leaves of each stalk of lemongrass and cut the thinner end at an angle to make lemongrass skewers. Place them in a tray of water to soak and set aside.

When the chicken has marinated, thread it onto the wet lemongrass skewers and grill over direct medium-high heat for 2 to 3 minutes per side, or until cooked through. Serves 4 to 6.

Niagara

BUSY BEE GARDENS
Open daily year round

Robert and Melissa Achal are two very energetic and passionate farmers. In their 15,000-square foot controlled greenhouse environment they maintain a Provencal climate to grow the most amazing organic lavender and other exotic plants like culinary saffron, lemongrass and Ontario's first edible geranium, the Attar of Rose. Busy Bee is Ontario's only manufacturer of food grade essential oils, distilling many plants into oils that you can use to enhance the flavour of baking and cooking. Just a few drops of rosemary, herbes de Provence, lavender and camomile essential oil add amazing flavours to cooking, baking, oils, vinegars and more. www.busybeegardens.com

758 Niagara Stone Road, Niagara-on-the-Lake

enjoy with
WAYNE GRETZKY
Unoaked Chardonnay
www.waynegretzkyestates.com

enjoy with
CHARLES BAKER
Riesling
www.charlesbaker.ca

pesto pan chicken

2 tablespoons (30 mL) Ontario canola oil
1 large onion, thinly sliced
4 thick slices artisan smoked bacon
1 red pepper, sliced
4 skinless, boneless free-range chicken
 breasts, cut into chunks
1 cup (250 mL) cherry tomatoes, halved
1/3 cup (80 mL) whipping cream
2 tablespoons (30 mL) basil pesto
1 cup (250 mL) baby spinach leaves
12 fresh basil leaves as garnish
Ontario salt

Heat the oil in a large skillet. Add the onions and bacon and cook for 5 minutes. Add chicken and cook, stirring occasionally until the chicken is cooked through, about 15 minutes.

Stir in the tomatoes and cook for 2 minutes. Pour the whipping cream over top and stir the pesto though the cream. Add spinach and warm through. Season well and scatter fresh basil leaves over top. Serves 4 to 6.

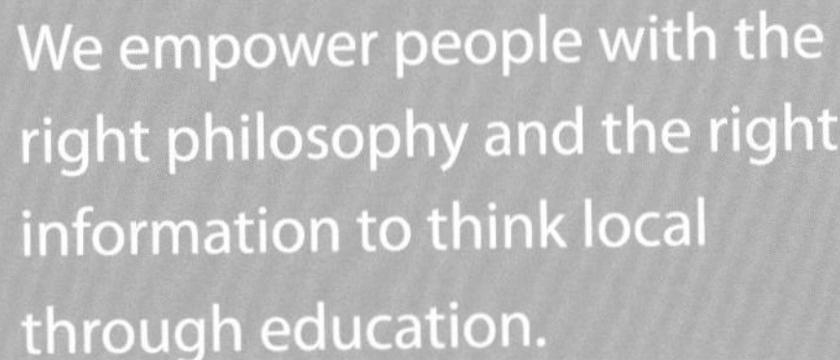

Prince Edward County

CARSON BAY FARMS
Farm gate sales

From busy career woman to farm girl, Marilyn Carson made the drastic change because she believes in good quality food. She and her husband Craig raise excellent Limousin beef, delicious turkeys, amazing chicken and of course, sell their farm fresh brown eggs. The home-grown chickens are raised naturally and are antibiotic free. Call for availability, 613-476-2952. www.carsonbayfarms.com

2967 Hwy 49, Picton

Ontario

ONTARIO GREENBELT

There has been so much controversy about Ontario's Greenbelt and like anything new, there will be people with opinions on either side of the concept. For me, I'm just thankful that someone has the vision to preserve our green space for generations to come. It means we'll have space to grow good food, we'll have lovely green spaces for us to enjoy and we'll be protecting essential resources. I can't imagine New York City without Central Park and now, I can't imagine Ontario without our Greenbelt.

www.greenbelt.ca

prosciutto wrapped quail

6 fresh quail
16 fresh sage leaves
8 thin slices prosciutto
4 tablespoons (60 mL) Ontario canola oil
2 tablespoons (30 mL) country fresh butter
1/2 cup (125 mL) dry white wine
1 teaspoon (5 mL) country fesh butter, chilled
Ontario salt

Pre-heat oven to 350F (180C). Place sage leaves inside each quail and season the inside well. Wrap each bird neatly with a slice of prosciutto, ensuring the seam is at the bottom.

Heat the canola oil and half the butter in a frying pan, just large enough to hold the 8 quail. When the oil is sizzling, put the birds in breast side down and sear them for 3 to 4 minutes. Turn over and brown the other side for another 3 to 4 minutes. Transfer the birds to an oven-proof dish and bake for 10 to 12 minutes.

Meanwhile, pour off all but 1 tablespoon of the oil and butter remaining in the fry pan, keeping any brown bits sticking to the bottom of the pan. Turn the heat to high and carefully add the white wine and reduce by half, scraping the bottom of the pan. Turn off the heat and swirl in cold butter, until it melts and thickens, making for a richer, silkier sauce. Serve quail warm from the oven with pan sauce. Serves 6.

enjoy with
PELEE ISLAND WINERY
Pinot Grigio
www.peleeisland.com

local food in

Sudbury & Algoma

Surprisingly the food scene in Sudbury and Algoma has deep roots. Families of every ethic diversity came to the north to work the mines bringing with them varying ways to weave their garden produce into the fabric of everyday life.

WILD FOOD

Blueberries grow wild throughout the region and to ask someone for their favourite picking spot is like asking someone where their favourite fishing hole is. The best patches are considered sacred ground. Many people actually leave work during blueberry season just to pick and sell blueberries. You can find them ready picked at roadside stands along the back roads.

Potatoes are a crop that grows abundantly in the Sudbury region and some of them are award winners! Both Anton Wiebe and Sheldon Falconer, from Anton Wiebe Ltd. of MacGregor were named first place winners in the McCain Champion Growers competition. In Sturgeon Falls, Larry's Chip Stand is a legend for chips that in 1953 sold for 10 cents. Today, Larry's daughter owns the stand and has earned her own reputation with amazing poutine that draws customers for miles around – definitely worth the visit.

QUAINT VILLAGES

Killarney is a beautiful port town on Georgian Bay and its known for its fresh fish and chips. Plenty of pickerel and whitefish are caught along the shores that stretch from Killarney to Manitoulin. They take the fresh catch of the day, lightly batter it and pair it up with their prize winning potatoes in a truly local dish. Killarney is one of those beautiful little towns that offer so many surprises. Make sure you stay awhile for the sunsets that shine a coppery pink on the La Cloche mountains.

ARTISAN FARMERS

Drive along the back roads and you'll be surprised at the delicious discoveries. In Iron Bridge, Sharon and Ken Lane run a farm called Grandpa's Dream Worm Farm. They're open all year and through the different seasons you'll find lots of fresh produce, from lettuce and tomatoes to melons and sweet corn. It's also a place popular with area fishermen, but you may have guessed that from its name!

This region is an area that draws fishermen from around the world. Fresh fish is caught from the crisp, cold waters of the north while First Nations fishermen offer smoked or fresh whitefish (the best come from Lake Superior).

The area throughout the North Shore has the characteristic Ontario sweet tooth for their beloved maple syrup and honey products. On St. Joseph Island alone, there are more than 80,000 trees tapped. They call maple season the 'rite of late winter and early spring' and celebrate it with a Maple Syrup Festival complete with boiling sap (sweet water), pancake breakfasts and sugar bush tours.

REGIONAL SPECIALTY

Porketta is a specialty of Sudbury. Rolled pork roast baked until fork tender is a signature dish. You can actually play Porketta Bingo at the Beef'N Bird Tavern, a favourite haunt of locals. And guess what the winner gets? Yes, steaming helpings of succulent porketta.

Nearly 40% of Sudbury's population is French speaking, so it's no surprise that you can find sugar pie and butter tarts plentiful in this region. If you're there, you'll have to go to Grandmother's Pie Shoppe. They're known for the best butter tarts in the northern region.

Sudbury and Algoma have a local food web directory, agriculture and culinary map, farmers' markets and lots of markets on farms that offer fresh food in season.

Eat Local Sudbury | www.eatlocalsudbury.com
Buy Algoma, Buy Fresh | www.buyalgoma.ca

sage & sausage cornbread stuffed turkey

1 10 lb Hayter's turkey
1 tablespoon (15 mL) Ontario canola oil
1 onion, chopped
2 garlic cloves, minced
1 pound (.45 kg) mushrooms, quartered
1/2 pound (.25 kg) loose sausage meat
1/4 cup (50 mL) country fresh butter
3 stalks celery, chopped
10 cups (2.5 L) day old cornbread, cubed
2 tablespoons (30 mL) dried sage
1 teaspoon (5 mL) dried thyme
1 cup (250 mL) chicken stock
Ontario salt

Preheat the oven to 450F (230C). In large skillet, heat oil over medium heat, sauté the onions, garlic, mushrooms and sausage, stirring occasionally, until sausage is fully cooked, about 10 minutes. Drain if necessary. Add butter and celery and season well. Cook until celery is soft, about 5 minutes.

In large bowl, add cornbread cubes, sage, thyme and the cooked sausage mixture. Add stock and toss to combine. Stuff the turkey cavity loosely. Place stuffed turkey breast side up in a roasting pan. Place in the oven and immediately reduce the heat to 350F (180C). Cook 20 minutes per pound.

Bake remaining stuffing in a baking dish, covered with foil, for 30 minutes. Uncover and bake until golden and crisp, about 10 minutes.

Huron County

HAYTER'S TURKEY
Open Monday to Saturday 9 to 6, Sunday 11 to 4

Third generation turkey farmer Dave Maguire and his family run a farm in Huron County that produces over 350,000 turkeys. Not only do they raise the beautiful white birds but they produce some delicious turkey products including sausage, pepperettes and burgers, so consumers can enjoy the lean goodness of turkey more often. Because everything is done on-site, from raising the birds to harvesting and processing, Hayter's turkeys are fresher and more flavourful. Look for Hayter's Farm products on your grocers' shelves as well as at their on-farm retail shop. www.haytersfarm.com, www.huronperthfarmtotable.ca

37467 Dashwood Road, Dashwood

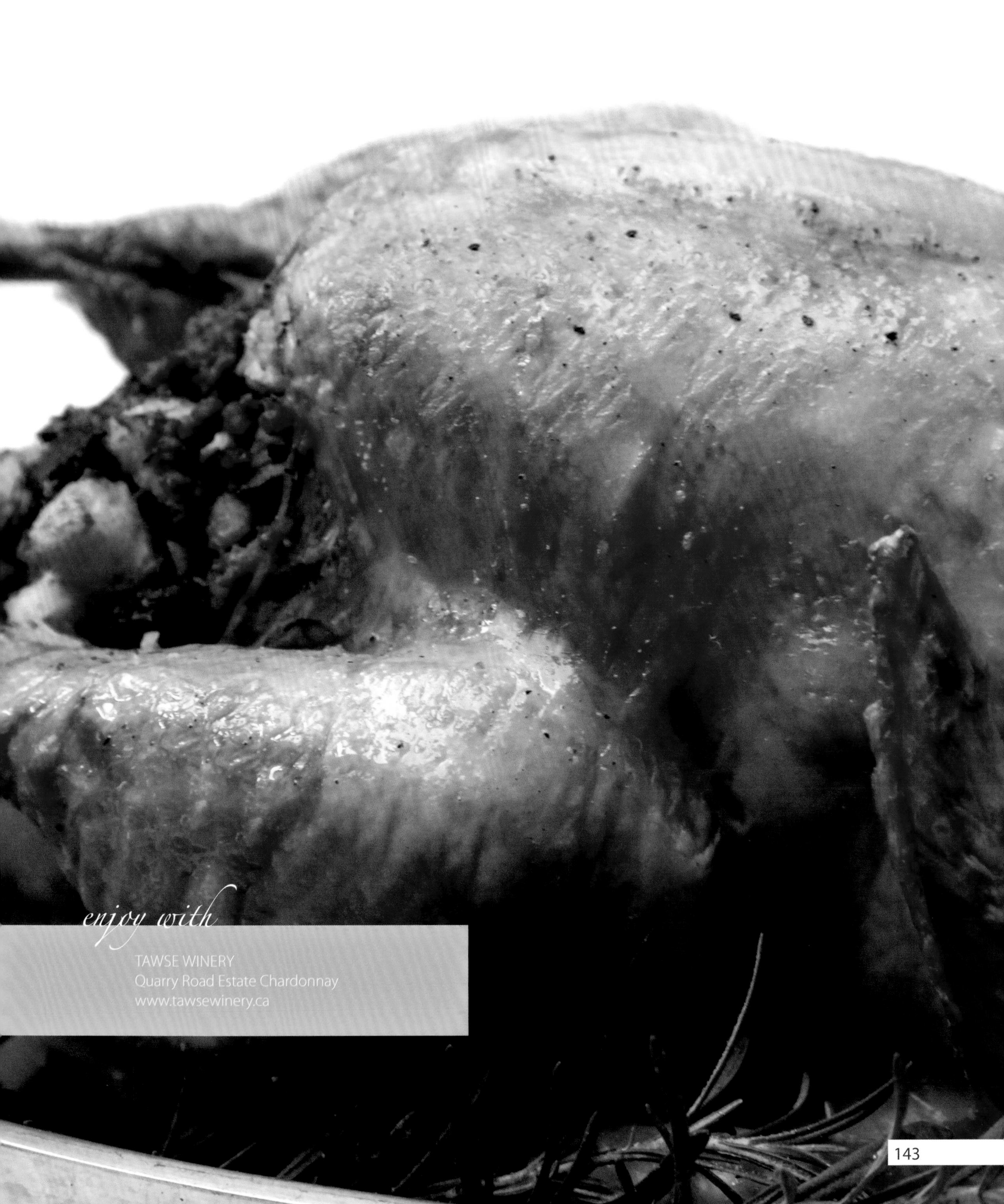
enjoy with
TAWSE WINERY
Quarry Road Estate Chardonnay
www.tawsewinery.ca

enjoy with

PELLER ESTATES
Pinot Noir
www.peller.com

vodka chicken

4 Ontario chicken breasts, skinless, boneless
1 cup (250 mL) all-purpose flour
2 tablespoons (30 mL) Ontario canola oil
2 shallots, minced
2 garlic cloves, minced
3 dried chili peppers
1/2 cup (125 mL) Prince Igor Vodka
1 cup (250 mL) chicken broth
3 tablespoons (45 mL) Ontario tomato sauce
1 vine ripened tomato, diced
1/4 cup (60 mL) Ontario parmesan cheese
1/2 cup (125 mL) whipping cream
Ontario salt

Trim chicken breasts of any fat. Season flour with salt and whisk to mix thoroughly. Heat the oil in a large skillet over medium high heat. Dredge chicken breasts in seasoned flour and place in skillet. Cook until browned on both sides, about 2 minutes per side. Transfer to a platter and keep warm.

Reduce heat to medium and add shallots, garlic and chili peppers to skillet. Cook until shallots are soft, about 2 minutes. Add vodka and cook until vodka has almost evaporated, about 4 minutes. Add broth and tomato sauce and reduce by half again, another 4 minutes.

Finish the sauce by adding diced tomato, parmesan cheese and cream. Heat through, then return chicken breasts to the skillet and cook until done, about 5 minutes. Serves 4.

Norfolk County

PRISTINE GOURMET
Wholesale only

Jason Persall owns and operates a 4th generation family farm in southern Ontario with his wife Linda and two children, Benton and Emma. Together they grow cash crops of soy, wheat and corn on approximately 1,000 acres of farmland. In 2003, they had an idea to produce high quality, artisan oils from their own crops. They started Persall Fine Foods Co. and now make cold-pressed extra virgin canola oil, soybean oils and soy sauce for premium restaurants and gourmet retail markets. In addition to their line of farm-to-gourmet table products, Jason also offers wine vinegars, cooking wines and mustards. Check the store locator on their website for a store near you, www.pristinegourmet.com

1121 Villa Nova Road, Waterford

For every one person you see working at the market, another two are busy at work in the back of the farm. As many as 27,000 people in Ontario are directly involved in preparing and selling the food you find at the market.

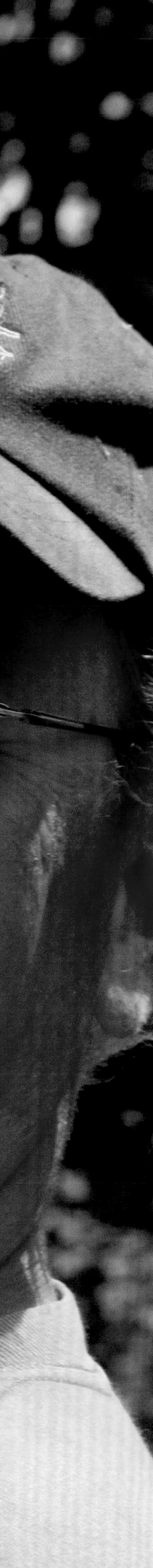

Pastured Meat

featuring

enjoy with
SOUTHBROOK VINEYARDS
Cabernet Rosé
www.southbrook.com

craig's honey ham

1 country-cured ham
2 bay leaves
1 onion, peeled
4 cloves
3 cups (750 mL) off-dry Ontario wine
3 tablespoons (45 mL) brown sugar
1 teaspoon (5 mL) ground cinnamon
1/2 teaspoon (2.5 mL) ground nutmeg
2 tablespoons (30 mL) Ontario honey
whole cloves

Soak the ham, covered for 24 to 30 hours in cold water. Drain. Place in a pot large enough to hold it with a close fitting lid. Tuck the bay leaves around the ham, add the onion, cloves, off-dry wine and enough water to cover.

Bring to a boil, cover and simmer very gently for 2 1/2 hours or until large bone in heavy end of ham becomes loose and protrudes. Lift the ham from the stock and place in a roasting pan to cool. Meanwhile, mix the brown sugar, cinnamon, nutmeg and honey to form a paste. As soon as the ham is cool enough to handle, remove the skin and with a sharp knife, make diagonal cuts 1/8-inch deep and 3/4-inch apart in the fat layer to make a diamond pattern. Rub in the honey paste and stud with cloves.

Preheat the oven to 375F (190C). Pour the cooking stock around the ham in the roasting pan to a depth of a 1/2-inch. Bake, basting occasionally for 20 to 30 minutes or until the coating looks crisp and golden. Serve hot or cold, sliced thinly with seasonal vegetables. Serves 6 to 8.

Sudbury

DALEW FARM
Community Shared Agriculture (CSA) and on-line sales

Dave and Chantal Lewington are absolutely adamant about their non-use of chemicals, artificial fertilizers and GMO feed on their farm. They grow a large variety of vegetables and raise pastured sheep, pigs and cattle. It all goes into the baskets for their large CSA program that services the North Bay and Sudbury area. To bring more local food to consumers they've started a Sudbury Eaters Buying Club. This allows consumers to simply order from the website whenever they need local food without the commitment of an annual CSA. www.dalewfarms.ca

10781 Hwy 64, Lavigne

hawberry cider lamb

1 leg of lamb
2 garlic cloves, sliced thinly
3 tablespoons (45 mL) Gypsey Shock & Haw Jam
1/2 cup (125 mL) apple cider
Ontario salt

Preheat oven to 450F (220C). Cut about 12 small slits into the flesh of the leg and insert the slices of garlic. Season the lamb and baste with hawberry jam. Place lamb fat side up in a roasting pan. Pour the apple cider into the pan.

Roast for 30 minutes, then turn the oven down to 350F (180C). Roast for an additional hour for medium, basting frequently with pan juices. Remove the lamb from the oven and let it rest in a warm place for 5 minutes before carving. Serves 4 to 6.

Note: if you can't get Gypsey Shock & Haw(berry) Jam, look for authentic Hawberry jam from Manitoulin Island

Manitoulin Island

GYPSY FAMILY FARM
On-farm market open late May to mid September

Ted Smith grew up on a market garden farm, so going back came naturally to this progressive farmer who grows an enormous variety of vegetables. At his Gore Bay Farmers' Market stand he hangs a sign that says "table of the bizarre and unusual" and that's exactly what some would call his vegetables. Multi-coloured carrots picked small and marketed as crayon carrots, cucumbers that look like russet potatoes and others that are round, fuzzy and striped are just some. Ted runs a Community Shared Agriculture (CSA) program for Manitoulin customers, sells at the Gore Bay Farmers' Market and from his on-farm stand. You'll also find lamb, free run eggs and a huge variety of jams, jellies, salsas and Hawberry gourmet preserves, many spiked with his favourite hot peppers. www.manitoulinfarmersmarket.com.

1065 Union Road, Evansville

enjoy with

RAVINE VINEYARDS
Reserve Merlot
www.ravinevineyard.com

Niagara has a local food web directory, agriculture and culinary map, 12 farmers' markets and lots of markets on farms that offer fresh food in season.

Niagara Culinary Trail | www.niagaraculinarytrail.com

local food in

Niagara

The Niagara escarpment runs through the region from east to west, creating a microclimate that changes the agricultural landscape dramatically north and south of it. North of the escarpment is Niagara tender fruit belt and wine country. South of the escarpment are apple orchards, chicken barns and cash crops.

Throughout its history, travellers would come from miles around to indulge in its tender fruit harvests; sexy peaches, luscious apricots, juicy cherries and succulent plums. Farm stands are everywhere, offering up the latest harvest, and restaurants design menus that complement the bounty of the region.

WINE REGION

Between the orchards and gardens are acres of vineyards. Niagara is Ontario's largest wine region, with a diverse assortment of wineries from small, family run operations to large international companies. All are unique in their own right. Some dry their grapes in tobacco kilns to concentrate flavours while others tend to increase quality in the vineyard with low yields. A few wineries are gravity fed, others are tucked away in caves, and some operate in a corner of a barn. This diversity makes Niagara an interesting destination for lovers of fine wines.

CULINARY ESSENTIALS

Niagara also produces some spectacular culinary products from the vineyard. Verjus is unfermented green grape juice with many uses from reduction sauces to salad dressings. Ice syrup is an unfermented and concentrated icewine juice that creates excitement when basted on grilled meats or used in a marinade. Both are culinary essentials.

Drive the back roads and chances are you'll find a farm vehicle loaded with produce. Follow it because it's most likely destined for a

restaurant. Go in, ask your server what's fresh and local and enjoy the goodness of the region.

FOOD & WINE

Niagara is filled with restaurants that use local food – from casual eateries to fine dining establishments. August Restaurant on King Street in Beamsville runs its kitchen on a 2-acre vegetable plot situated on a fruit farm nearby. It's a casual place with a real country feel. On the posh side is Peller Estate Winery Restaurant, with its house-made charcuterie and delicious wines. Inniskillin Wines, on the Niagara Parkway, has a culinary studio where they prepare many delicious local food dishes for guests who drop in, and a cooking school turned winery, The Good Earth creates fine wines to accompany their food strategies.

CULINARY ENTREPRENEURS

Niagara's culinary culture includes entrepreneurs like Mario Pingue, who brings his Italian craft of curing meats to create the best prosciutto in the province; the Kurtz Family who turn the harvests of their fruit farm into gourmet food products sold in their gourmet marketplace on the Niagara Parkway; Paul Moyer for his farm grown taffy apples and red fife wheat pasta; and Cherry Lane Farm where you can buy frozen fruit from the region year round.

Farmers in the region are also creatively expanding beyond the expected. The Fruit Shack in Niagara-on-the-Lake is growing big, black cherries under hoop; Whitty Farms focuses on traditional or heritage varieties of tomatoes that pack loads of flavour; and Busy Bee Gardens does the unexpected with the province's first saffron and lemon grass crops.

enjoy with
FOREIGN AFFAIR WINERY
Cabernet Sauvignon
www.foreignaffairwine.com

horseradish crusted rib roast

1/2 cup (125 mL) country fresh butter, softened
1 head of garlic, cloves coarsely chopped
1/2 cup (125 mL) prepared Ontario horseradish
3 tablespoons (45 mL) fresh thyme,
3 tablespoons (45 mL) fresh rosemary
3 tablespoons (45 mL) fresh sage, chopped
One 8-pound (3.63 kg) rib roast of beef
Ontario salt

Preheat the oven to 550F (280C). In a food processor, combine the butter with the garlic, horseradish, thyme, rosemary and sage and process to a paste. Refrigerate until ready to use.

Stand the roast in a very large roasting pan. Season generously all over and set it fatty side up. Spread the horseradish-herb butter in a thin layer all over the top. Transfer to oven and immediately reduce heat to 350F (180C). Bake for 18 to 20 minutes per pound for medium rare. Remove from oven and transfer the roast to a carving board to rest for at least 10 minutes before serving. Serves 4 to 6.

Peterborough County

WHOLEARTH FARMSTUDIO
Farm market store open seasonally

Montana Jones and Michael Caligiuri are having a love affair with the land. On their 100 acre farm, they raise heritage Tamworth pigs, organic heritage Angus cattle, heritage Shropshire lamb, all natural pastured chickens and they nurture a giant organic vegetable garden. From their harvests they offer a few CSA programs, some that are only vegetables, others for meats and some a combination of both. Their farm experience, Heritage Harvest Feast, is an amazing event that is as organic, natural and pastured as those who live on the farm. Internships also available. www.wholeearth.com

143 Concession Road 14, Hastings

Northumberland County

OSLANDS SHEEP & BEEF FARM
Open Tuesday to Thursday, 11 to 5, otherwise by chance

Cindy and Darrell Osland run a 240-acre farm in rural Port Hope. They're passionate about growing and raising the best, safest food they can for themselves and for their customers. To ensure that their beef and lamb are all naturally raised, the Oslands grow their own animal feed and use safe farming practices, with respectful animal care being their first and foremost concern. You can find the Oslands at the Port Hope Farmers' Market with plenty of vegetables, various cuts of lamb and beef as well as their popular patties and sausages. Don't forget to pick up a dozen farm fresh eggs.

4996 5th Line, Port Hope

icewine & balsamic glazed portobello beef

1/2 cup (125 mL) Ontario balsamic vinegar
1/2 cup (125 mL) icewine vinegar
1/4 cup (60 mL) brown sugar
2 tablespoons (30 mL) Ontario vegetable oil
4 large portobello mushrooms
4 tenderloin steaks, tied into rounds
Ontario salt
garden fresh rocket for garnish

In a small saucepan over high heat, add the vinegars and brown sugar. Stir until the sugar is dissolved, then cook for 6 minutes more or until slightly thickened and syrupy. Set aside to cool.

Meanwhile, preheat the oven to 450F (230C). Heat the oil in a large oven-proof skillet over medium heat. Add the whole mushrooms and cook for 5 minutes. Transfer to the oven and cook for 15 minutes. Set aside. Increase heat to high, sprinkle the steaks with salt and sear for 2 minutes each side. Transfer to the oven and cook for an additional 8 minutes for medium rare. Remove from oven and let rest for 10 minutes.

When ready to serve, lay a steak on a dinner plate and top with rocket. Top with a mushroom and drizzle with icewine glaze. Garnish with more rocket. Serves 4.

enjoy with

PILLITTERI ESTATES WINERY
Exclamation Reserve Merlot
www.pillitteri.com

enjoy with

CROWN BENCH ESTATE WINERY
Reserve Cabernet Sauvignon
www.crownbenchestates.com

lamb chops with kiwi compote

1 cup (250 mL) sugar
1/2 cup (125 mL) water
3 cups (750 mL) Niagara kiwi, stemmed and halved
2 teaspoons (10 mL) Niagara verjus
1 vanilla bean
1 teaspoon (5 mL) fennel seeds
1 cinnamon stick
8 Ontario lamb chops
1 tablespoon (15 mL) Ontario canola oil
Ontario salt

In a large saucepan combine the sugar and water. Slowly bring to a boil, stirring until the sugar is dissolved. Remove from the heat and add the kiwi and verjus. Tie the vanilla bean, fennel seeds and cinnamon stick in a cheesecloth and add to the pan. Let stand at room temperature for a few hours.

Bring to a boil, reduce heat to medium and simmer until thickened to a jam consistency, about 2 hours. Discard the cloth bag and ladle kiwi compote into a glass jar with a tight-fitting lid.

When ready to serve, season lamb on both sides. Warm oil in a large skillet over medium high heat and cook the lamb for 5 minutes, turning half way through. Serve with kiwi compote. Serves 4.

Ottawa

STANLEY'S OLDE MAPLE LANE FARM
Open weekends during maple season, February to April

Earl and Joy Stanley have a 250-acre farm in Edwards, a small community with the city limits of Ottawa. They tap a 70-acre sugar bush on the farm as well as two other off-site sugar bushes, one in London and the other in Hopetown. That's lots of maple syrup and it's all sold on their farm, either through their retail shop or in their banquet menus. During maple season they offer sleigh rides, sugar bush tours and more sweet fun on their beautiful country facilities that also hosts weddings and banquets all year long. www.stanleysfarm.com

2452 Yorks Corners Road, Edward

pecan-crusted rack of pork

1 4 pound (1.8 kg) Ontario rack of pork
2 tablespoons (30 mL) breadcrumbs
1/2 cup (125 mL) Northern pecans, finely ground
1 tablespoon (15 mL) fresh parsley, minced
2 tablespoons (30 mL) mustard
Ontario salt

Preheat oven to 450F (230C). Trim the meat around the bones, slice the top in a diamond pattern being careful not to penetrate to the meat. Season and set aside. In a bowl, place breadcrumbs, ground pecans, parsley, and salt. Mix well. Spread mustard over the fat side of the rack and spoon pecan mixture over top, pressing lightly with your fingers. Continue spooning pecan mixture over top and pressing it onto the pork until all of the pecan crumbs are used up.

Place the roast, fat side up in a roasting pan and roast for 1 hour. Tent the roast with aluminum foil and continue to roast for an additional hour. Remove from oven and let rest for 10 minutes before carving. Serves 4.

Wellington Guelph

BLUE HAVEN FARM
Farmers' Market sales

John and Marcia Stevers' family farm is tucked away on 10 acres, less than 100 km west of Toronto. They humanely raise, 'fresh-air-style' pastured, hormone and antibiotic free animals. Among their unique and rare birds are heritage turkey, Guinea fowl, pheasants, ducks (Muscovy and Jumbo Pekins). They have heritage Tamworth pigs, Jacob sheep and goats. The Stevers grow 2 main crops, Jerusalem artichokes and garlic and because they believe in their community, they sell products from over 120 local farm families; the list includes maple syrup, rhubarb, herbs, beef, rabbit, grains, jams, baked goods and more. You can find them at the Guelph Farmers' Market. www.bluehavenfarm.moonfruit.com

6089 4th Line, Rockwood

enjoy with
HILLEBRAND
Trius Red
www.hillebrand.com

local food in

Prince Edward County

Only a county steeped in good taste would boast its own Taste Trail. Follow the clearly marked Taste Trail road signs and you'll find the best farms, wineries, restaurants and food shops this quaint county has to offer.

You'll find Prince Edward County Lavender in Hillier and Lakeshore Farms Market in Wellington. Bloomfield has a mushroom farm, cattle ranches and an amazing artisan ice cream called Slickers; ask for their Apple Pie Ice Cream, rumour has it that an entire apple pie goes into each batch of ice cream!

FESTIVALS

The folks in 'The County' as it's known to the locals, love to celebrate the abundance with which they're so blessed during festivals like Maple In The County, Taste and Countylicious. Countylicious (www.countylicious.ca), held every spring and fall, is an opportunity to experience fine County cuisine at farm and country prices. Taste (www.tastecelebration.ca) is an amazing weeklong culinary event held in September, with cooking demos, sommelier-led wine tours, harvest parties and entertainment.

My favourite is Harvestin' the County (www.harvestin.ca) because the inspiration came from the joy of celebrating and supporting the local agricultural community – do you need any other reason? A long table is simply set down the main street in Wellington and hundreds of people come out to enjoy a supper designed from a 100% locally grown menu. I wouldn't miss it, and if you're a true foodie, you wouldn't either.

COOKERY SCHOOL

The Waring House Restaurant, Inn & Cookery School is on County Road 1, just west of Picton. The cooking school offers hands-on, recreational cooking classes year round, complete with farm tours, while the Inn's menu reflects the wonderful variety of produce and other agricultural and fisheries products found in The County. Adjacent to the Waring House property is Hagerman's Farm. Lyle Hagerman makes regular trips to the Inn and keeps their refrigerators stocked with fresh local produce.

BEER

Prince Edward County was the grain basket of Canada, exporting barley and hops in huge volumes to markets across Canada, the U.S. and England. Barley Days Brewery was founded on this rich agricultural history, and today you'll find some barley and hops replanted for the brewing industry.

WINE

But barley and hops have long been replaced with grapes as Prince Edward County is Ontario's fastest-growing wine region, with internationally acclaimed wines the likes of Norm Hardie and Long Dog.

CHEESE

Not surprisingly, the County is also home to North America's 'greenest' dairy, Fifth Town Artisan Cheese Company. They source fresh, local goat and sheep milk and use traditional methods of crafting cheeses. The LFP certified cheeses include chevre, feta, whey ricotta and a full line of indescribably delicious specialty cheeses. You can find their cheeses at specialty shops throughout Ontario and at the dairy.

Prince Edward County has a local food web directory, agriculture and culinary map, farmers' markets and lots of markets on farms that offer fresh food in season.

Harvest in the County | www.harvestin.ca

Taste the County Prince Edward | www.tastethecounty.ca

Perth County

PERTH PORK PRODUCTS
Call ahead to purchase, 519-393-6846

Fred de Martines loves pigs of all kinds, especially heritage breeds like Tamworth, Berkshire, Iron Age and Wild Boar. "People who are interested in heritage breeds are interested in food," Fred explains. The pigs are raised "the old fashioned way" on the 100-acre farm. The animals are fed vegetable scraps from the local restaurants, a program run by the local YMCA and the wild boar enjoy a diet of feed complemented with whole walnuts collected from trees throughout the county. In 2009, Fred was awarded the distinction of Magister Porcarius by the World Slow Food Movement and the Tamworth pig was inducted into the Canadian Slow Food Movement's Ark of Taste. You can buy Perth Pork Products at the farm or go to www.perthporkproducts.com

4538 Line 38, Sebringville

pork patties with nectarine relish

1/4 small red onion, diced
1 ripe nectarine, diced
1 tablespoon (15 mL) Ontario honey
1 tablespoon (15 mL) Niagara verjus
light dusting of cayenne pepper
1 pound (.45 kg) ground pork
1 farm fresh egg
1/2 cup (125 mL) seasoned breadcrumbs
handful of fresh parsley, minced
1 tablespoon (15 mL) Ontario canola oil
Ontario salt

Soak onions for 10 minutes in ice water. Drain and return to the bowl. Add nectarines, honey, verjus and cayenne pepper. Season with salt. Let stand 15 minutes or if storing, cover and refrigerate up to 1 day.

In a large bowl, mix the pork, egg, breadcrumbs, parsley, and salt well. Form into mini patties. Warm canola oil in a skillet over medium heat. Add pork patties and cook until browned on one side, about 4 minutes. Turn over and cook for an additional 5 minutes. Alternately, heat grill to medium-high and lightly oil grates. Grill, turning once, until cooked through, 10 to 12 minutes. Serve warm topped with nectarine and red onion relish.

Chatham-Kent County

THOMPSONS LIMITED
Not open to the public

You may recognize the bags of Thompsons dried beans on your local grocers' shelves. These beans come from a family-run business headquartered in Blenheim with over a dozen more locations scattered throughout Ontario, including Hensall, the Bean Capital of Ontario. It was Bob Thompson's grandfather who started the company in 1924 and today there are 7 Thompsons working in the family business from brothers to cousins. They process the beans that go into their bags and provide custom labelled beans for private companies and for canning factories such as the Unico brand in Essex County. Ontario beans to watch out for are Red and White Kidney Beans, Yellow Eye Beans and White Pea Beans (or Navy Beans). www.thompsonslimited.com

2 Hyland Drive, Blenheim

enjoy with

SANDBANKS ESTATE WINERY
Baco Noir 10th Selection
www.sandbankswinery.com

roast pork with rosemary white beans

1 pound (.45 kg) dried Ontario white beans
1 onion, peeled and quartered
3 cloves garlic, peeled and chopped
2 bay leaves
2 cups (500 mL) Ontario dry white wine
2 cups (500 mL) chicken broth
water to cover
One 4-pound (1.81 kg) pork loin roast
with a generous layer of fat
1/3 cup (80 mL) Ontario canola oil
6 large garlic cloves
2 sprigs fresh rosemary
3/4 cup (180 mL) Ontario dry white wine
3 slices artisan pork belly, diced
6 garlic cloves, minced
3 sprigs fresh rosemary, minced
half an onion, minced
Ontario salt

Rinse beans well and place in a large pot. Fill the pot with water to cover by at least 4 inches and set aside to soak overnight. When ready to cook, drain the beans and return to the pot.

Add onion, garlic, bay leaves, wine and broth to the pot. If wine and broth have not covered the beans, add enough wine or water to cover the beans by 2 to 3 inches. Slowly bring the beans to a boil, reduce to a simmer and continue to simmer the beans until they're tender, about 2 hours. As the liquid boils away, add more water. Test the beans for doneness periodically to prevent overcooking. Drain well.

Meanwhile, score the fat on top of the loin in a crosshatch pattern, without cutting into the flesh.

In a small food processor, add oil, garlic and rosemary. Pulse until minced well. Rub the herb mixture into the slits in the pork and over the entire surface of the loin. Preheat the oven to 450F (225C).

Put the pork loin in a roasting pan just large enough to hold the meat, fat side up. Pour the wine in the roasting pan and roast for 20 minutes. Reduce the oven temperature to 300F (150C) and roast for 1 1/2 to 2 hours or until pork is fork tender.

In a large skillet, cook the pork belly for 3 minutes. Add garlic, onion and rosemary and cook until onions are soft. Add the cooked beans and mix well. Drizzle with oil and keep warm. Remove pork from oven and strain pan juices into the beans. Season and mix well. Spoon onto a large platter. Top with roast and serve warm.

Use this book by asking what's coming out of the garden this week. What can I look for next week? Think like a farmer and think of the seasons, it's the only way to cook.

flank steak with chimichuri sauce

2 to 3 pounds (.91 - 1.36 kg) Ontario flank steak
3 tablespoons (45 mL) Ontario soy sauce
2 tablespoons (30 mL) Niagara verjus
2 tablespoons (30 mL) Ontario canola oil
2 tablespoons (30 mL) maple syrup
1 garlic clove, crushed
1/4 red onion, minced
3 garlic cloves
1/2 teaspoon (2.5 mL) red pepper flakes
1/2 cup (125 mL) fresh parsley or half a bunch
2 tablespoons (30 mL) fresh oregano
1/4 cup (60 mL) Ontario extra virgin canola oil
2 tablespoons (30 mL) Ontario vinegar
Ontario salt

Put the flank steak in a shallow dish just large enough to hold it snugly. Whisk the soy sauce, verjus, canola oil, maple syrup and garlic together. Season well with salt and pour over steak. Cover and marinate for 1 to 2 hours.

To make the Chimichuri sauce, put the remaining ingredients in a food processor and pulse until well incorporated. Place the flank steak on a broiler pan and broil for 6 to 8 minutes per side. Remove from oven and let rest for 10 minutes. Slice diagonally and serve warm with Chimichurri sauce. Serves 4 to 6.

Toronto

ROWE FARMS
Open daily, check website for hours

Rowe Farms is a cooperative of farmers led by internationally-acclaimed farmer Roger Harley. Roger's farming philosophy is to farm economically in an environment that supports animal welfare; meaning the animals graze freely, eating plants not feed. This means the Rowe Farm philosophy does not include engineered animal proteins, antibiotics or growth hormones They offer a full variety of healthy products from beef, chicken, lamb, pork and farm fresh eggs to cured products such as sausages and patties. You can buy Rowe Farms meats at their 5 retail locations, at specialty food stores like Highland Farms, Fiesta Farms, the Organic Garage and Fortino's. www.rowefarms.ca

912 Queen Street E, Toronto
2126 Queen Street E, Toronto
2230 Bloor Street W, Toronto
105 Roncesvalles Avenue, Toronto
St Lawrence Farmers' Market
1027 Gordon Street, Guelph

enjoy with
INNISKILLIN WINES
Three Vineyards Pinot Noir
www.inniskillin.com

enjoy with
LEGENDS ESTATE WINERY
Shiraz Reserve
www.legendsestates.com

veal shoulder with caramelized shallots

6 pound (2.72 kg) veal shoulder roast
1 pound (.45 kg) shallots, peeled
2 teaspoons (10 mL) Ontario maple syrup
2 teaspoons (10 mL) Ontario icewine vinegar
Ontario salt

Preheat oven to 500F (250C). Season veal well. Place in a large roasting pan, roast for 15 minutes. Reduce oven temperature to 350F (180C) and place shallots around the pork. Roast for 1 hour, turning shallots with tongs after about 30 minutes.

Transfer veal to a platter and tent loosely with foil. Add maple syrup and vinegar to the roasting pan with shallots and cook over medium heat, shaking the pan to coat shallots. Cook until syrupy and shallots begin to brown, about 5 minutes.

Transfer shallots to a shallow bowl. Toss with vinegar and season. Cover with foil to keep warm. Serve veal with shallots, drizzling any extra liquid over veal. Serves 4 to 6.

Holland Marsh

SINGH FARM FRESH
Farmers' Market sales

Shane and Jenn Singh are proud owners of their 32-acre farm in the Holland Marsh. Following in his dad's footsteps, Shane grows different lettuces, beets, and a variety of other vegetables. I found Shane and his irresistible produce at the Bradford Farmers' Market. The quality and freshness of what he displayed drew me to him immediately. Everything Shane brings to market is picked that morning so you can't get any fresher than that. You can also find him at the Distillery District Farmers' Market and since his farm is adjacent to Canal Road Farmers' Market, you can simply drop in there for some of Singh's fresh produce.

1153 Canal Road, Bradford

The fresh foods of the province are sought after by innovative chefs. They create amazing dishes that depend as much on the production of their ingredients as they do on the transformation of those ingredients into a delicious dish.

Field Vegetables: pick of the crop

featuring

enjoy with

HENRY OF PELHAM FAMILY ESTATE
Cuvée Catharine Brut
www.henryofpelham.com

spring onion tart

1/2 pound (.23 g) small new potatoes
4 slices smoky artisan bacon, diced
1 recipe essential savoury tart shell, page 297
3 farm fresh eggs
1/2 cup (125 mL) half and half cream
1/2 cup (125 mL) Ontario gouda cheese, grated
2 tablespoons (30 mL) wholegrain mustard
1 bunch of garden spring onions, trimmed
and halved lengthways
Ontario salt

Place the potatoes in a saucepan and cover with cold, salted water. Bring to the boil and simmer for 10 minutes or until tender. Drain well and set aside to cool. While the potatoes are cooking, sauté the bacon in a skillet until crisp. Drain on paper towels

Preheat the oven to 400 F (200C). Slice the cooled potatoes into thin slices and arrange in the base of the cooled tart shell. Beat the eggs, cream, cheese, mustard and bacon in a bowl and season to taste. Arrange the spring onions on top. Pour over the egg mixture and cook for 25 minutes until set but still a bit wobbly. It will set further as it cools. Let stand for 5 minutes, then slice and serve.

Northumberland County

WICKLOW WAY FARM
Open weekends only in season

It's one of the most beautiful and romantic gardens in Ontario. Elaina Asselin and Gregory Hill are farmers who tend to three acres of raised beds that are perfectly weeded, all manicured and growing certified organic heirloom tomatoes and market garden vegetables. Last count, they had over 150 different varieties of heirloom tomatoes, 30 varieties of lettuce, colourful beets, carrots and French beans. You can find Wicklow tomatoes in Toronto at Harvest Wagon (Yonge and Summerhill) and at Golden Orchard in the St. Lawrence Market. They offer a 16-week CSA (Community Shared Agriculture) program and in the spring they sell heirloom vegetable plants to aspiring gardeners. www.wicklowway.ca

188 Lakeport Road, Colborne

enjoy with

WILLOW SPRINGS WINERY
Awesome Blossom Rosé
www.willowspringswinery.com

asparagus & beans

2 tablespoons (30 mL) extra-virgin Ontario canola oil
1 large onion, sliced
1 pound (.45 kg) asparagus, trimmed and
chopped into bite-sized pieces
3 garlic cloves, minced
1 tablespoon (15 mL) dried oregano
1/2 teaspoon (2.5 mL) Ontario red pepper flakes
1 19-ounce can (540 mL) red kidney beans
Ontario balsamic vinegar
Ontario salt

Heat the oil in a large skillet. Add the onion and cook until just softened, about 2 minutes. Add the asparagus, garlic, oregano and red pepper flakes and season well. Sauté until asparagus softens, approximately 4 minutes. Drain the kidney beans and add to the skillet and continue to sauté until beans are warmed through and the asparagus is still al dente, approximately 3 minutes. Spoon warm onto 2 dinner plates and drizzle with a bit of balsamic vinegar. Serves 2 as a main meal or 4 to 6 as a first course.

Norfolk County

SPEARIT FARM
On-farm sales open seasonally from early May to end of June

Brenda and Raymond Lamens have worked their 300-acre asparagus farm for 30 years. Even though many of their neighbours were growing tobacco, the Lamens knew right from the beginning that their well-draining, sandy loam was perfect for asparagus. Today the Lamens grow 50 acres of densely planted asparagus and Brenda works closely with the University of Guelph to develop the best tasting varieties for the Ontario climate. The remaining farm is planted to corn and soybeans. Even though each asparagus crop goes to the wholesale market, those who know can buy directly from the Lamens' farm.

1700 North Road, Langton

baked cauliflower and pancetta

farm fresh butter, room temperature
1/2 cup (125 mL) fresh breadcrumbs
1/2 cup (125 mL) Ontario parmesan cheese
4 slices pancetta, cooked and crumbled
1 tablespoon (15 mL) fresh parsley, chopped
5 cups (1.25 L) cauliflower florets
2 teaspoons (10 mL) farm fresh butter, melted
Ontario salt

Preheat oven to 350F (180C). Smear the base of an 8-inch square casserole dish with butter. Set aside. In a bowl, mix the breadcrumbs, parmesan cheese, pancetta and parsley together. Season well and set aside.

Cut the cauliflower into medium, even-sized florets and cook in lightly-salted water for 5 minutes. Drain immediately and toss with half the breadcrumb mixture. Arrange in a single layer in the buttered dish. Add melted butter to remaining breadcrumb mixture and sprinkle over top. Bake for 25 minutes or until edges begin to brown. Serve hot. Serves 4 to 6.

Niagara

NIAGARA FOOD SPECIALTIES
Wholesale only

Brothers Mario and Fernando Pingue have taken over the family business from their father, specializing in prosciutto and other Italian-style cured meats. Some of the ham aging in the cellars is from heritage breeds of pigs; Tamworth, Berkshire and a hybrid Tamworth, Wild Boar breed. Others come from drug-free (no antibiotics or growth hormones) Duroc or Landrace animals that have not been been fed any animal byproducts. The Pingues use Local Food Plus (LFP) certified animals explaining that natural animal husbandry is the first criteria for Pingue products. www.pingueprosciutto.com

6893 Oakwood Drive, Niagara Falls

barbecued corn with herb butter

1/2 cup (125 mL) farm fresh butter, room temperature
1/3 cup (80 mL) finely chopped fresh herbs like
basil, rosemary, chives, oregano and thyme
1/2 teaspoon (2.5 mL) Ontario salt
8 ears of fresh corn

Mix butter, herbs and salt together in a food processor until smooth. Transfer to a bowl and set aside. Remove just a few of the outer layers of cornhusks on each corn cob. Fold back remaining husks and remove corn silk. Spread herbed butter on corn kernels and rewrap inner husks around corn. Turn the barbecue to medium high heat. Grill until husks are slightly charred and corn is tender, turning often, about 20 minutes.
Oven method: Put buttered corn in a preheated 350F (180C) oven. Bake 10 to 12 minutes. Remove from oven and serve warm. Serves 4 to 6.

Durham County

COOPER'S CSA FARM & CORN MAZE
On-farm market open seasonally from Wednesday to Sunday

Steve and Lisa Cooper run one of Ontario's largest CSA (Community Shared Agriculture) programs from their 100-acre farm. They grow over 50 different vegetables from asparagus to zucchini and with some of them, they offer up to 50 different varieties. That's a huge variety of vegetables! The CSA began in 2007 with a few families and today the Coopers serve about 500 families with their farm fresh veggies. The Coopers also run an on-farm market, attend the Farmers' Markets at Newmarket, Aurora, Uxbridge and Stowville and still run the most recognizable road-side farm stand on Yonge Street in Newmarket. Congratulations Steve and Lisa for winning the title, Canada's Outstanding Young Farmer for 2010.
www.coopersfarm.ca

266 Ashworth Road, Zephyr

It is in our agricultural community, where we find the most valuable resources, the greatest intensity of flavours and the purest of produce.

Toronto has 19 farmers' markets that offer fresh food in season and many artisan food shops stocking local products.

local food in

Toronto

Toronto is often referred to as the big city or the concrete jungle and those names would amuse anyone interested in local food. To a locavore, Toronto, is in fact, a city of urban farmers, amazing farmers' markets, delicious farm-to-table events and the gathering place for local food.

The St. Lawrence Farmers' Market began more than 200 years ago and today, more than 50 farmers and producers bring their seasonal produce to the market that spills out of the giant building into a 10,000 square foot market warehouse across the road.

Toronto is the largest retail market offering farmers more than two million potential customers. This mass of population has inspired some farmers, like Mark Trealout of the Kawartha Ecological Growers (KEG), to consolidate the produce from more than 20 growers in his region and bring it to the farmers' markets in the big city.

LOCAL FOOD RETAILER

Culinarium (www.culinarium.ca) is a small artisan food shop that serves as a community centre for locavores. The shop showcases what's available in Ontario for folks who love local foods, and they run cooking seminars focusing on local foods, teaching their customers, for example, how to substitute maple syrup for sugar in recipes.

COMMUNITY GARDENS

Evergreen is a charitable organization that makes city living more livable by encouraging community gardens and urban farming. They run the Evergreen Brickworks Farmers' Market (Saturday mornings) and host the Brickworks Picnic. This event, organized by Slow Food Toronto, has become one of Ontario's most amazing farm-to-table events, with more than 50 farmers and chefs pairing to showcase local food.

Toronto has more community gardens per capita than any other city in Ontario. Community gardens are so hot in the big city that it has given birth to new businesses to support the renewed and

growing interest in growing your own food. Young Urban Farmers (www.youngurbanfarmers.com) is a company that will set up your garden, maintain it and harvest it for a fee. They also sell raised beds in any size and self watering pots for absentee gardeners. The Backyard Urban Farm Company (www.bufco.ca) designs, builds, installs and maintains organic vegetable gardens for homes, schools, corporate spaces, daycare centres and retirement facilities.

In the spring, Hart House at the University of Toronto is home to Seedy Saturday, one-stop shopping for the very best seeds and gardening advice. Growing your own food is not new to some; the Royal York Hotel has had a rooftop garden for the past 14 years. The gardens are next to the beehives and together the food serves the hotel restaurant with some of its fresh vegetables, herbs and honey.

LOCAL FOOD CERTIFICATION

Toronto is home to Local Foods Plus (LFP, www.localfoodplus.ca), an organization that certifies growers in the areas of production, labour, native habitat preservation, animal welfare and on-farm energy use, and leverages these standards to open new higher-value markets for Ontario farmers. Look for growers that are LFP certified. Some say like VQA (Vintners Quality Alliance), it's a sign of great quality.

RESTAURANTS

There is a growing number of small restaurants that buy and cook local food not because it's in fashion, but because they've simply found it to be the best in flavour and quality. Marben on Wellington Avenue West is run by butcher, Ryan Donovan and chef, Carl Heinrich. They buy whole animals and deliciously use every piece of it. At Torito Tapas Bar on Augusta you'll find authentic Spanish dishes created with the best local ingredients and chef Rocco Agostino uses local food to cook authentic Italian dishes in his restaurant Enoteca Sociale in Toronto's west end.

In this hectic mad world we live in today we often lose sight of the very essence that promotes our health and well being. The goodness that comes from the earth, offered to us in its own time.

enjoy with
COYOTE'S RUN
Red Paw Vineyard Pinot Gris
www.coyotesrunwinery.com

tomato basil tart

2-1/2 ounces (70 g) Ontario chevre, room temperature
3 tablespoons (45 mL) fresh garden pesto
1 recipe essential savoury tart shell, page 297
about 48 red and/or yellow cherry tomatoes
Ontario salt
basil leaves for garnish, shredded

Mix the goat cheese and pesto together. Season and spread it on the bottom of the cooled tart. Fit a circle of cherry tomatoes around the outside of the tart. Continue to fill the tart with cherry tomatoes, alternating colours if possible, until the entire tart is filled with cherry tomatoes.

Bake for an additional 25 minutes or until filling bubbles. Remove from oven and allow to cool. Garnish with fresh shredded basil. Makes 1 tart.

Holland Marsh

CANAL ROAD FARM MARKET
Open from mid June to mid October or later

Dave and John Teichroeb are brothers who recently purchased an 8.5 acre farm on the banks of the Holland Marsh canal. They both run the busy fresh farm market and lease out the surrounding acreage to another farmer who grows a variety of vegetables including red and green leaf lettuce, romaine, carrots, beets, leeks and more. You'll find this produce inside the market along with more fresh fruit and vegetables from within the Holland Marsh. The soil in the Holland Marsh is rich, black velvet and the vegetables that grow in it are absolutely delicious!

252 Canal Road, Bradford

ONTARIO BEER

Hops once grew wherever beer was brewed in Ontario. After decades of moving away from growing hops as a viable Ontario crop, the Ontario hops industry is experiencing a rebirth with a new generation of farmers nurturing a crop that was almost forgotten in this province.

Canada's only teaching brewery at Niagara College is planting their own hops this year on the Niagara-on-the-Lake campus. While they wait for their first crop, Brewmaster Professor Jon Downing names off local growers who are just beginning to grow hops in Vineland, Guelph, Bloomfield and Niagara-on-the-Lake.

There are over 65 craft brewers in Ontario and with a revival of hops crops and barley malters segregating Ontario barley, it won't be long before we can claim some Ontario beers are truly local.

www.ontariocraftbrewers.com

garlic and thyme braised cauliflower

4 mini farmers' cauliflower
4 heads of garlic, top sliced to expose the cloves
1/2 cup (125 mL) dry white Ontario wine
2 cups (500 mL) chicken stock
8 sprigs thyme
2 tablespoons (30 mL) country fresh butter
Ontario salt

In a large stock pot, put cauliflower, garlic, wine, chicken broth and enough water to cover. Bring to a boil and boil for 15 minutes.

Preheat oven to 350F (180C). Drain, reserving 1 cup (250 mL) of cooking liquid and place cauliflower and garlic in an ovenproof skillet. Pour the reserved cooking liquid over the cauliflower. Add thyme and bake for 20 minutes.

Remove cauliflower from the dish. Add the butter to the pan juices and whisk to combine. Spoon the pan juices over the cauliflower and serve. Serves 4 to 6.

Eating should never be boring and then cooking will never be.

Niagara

INN THE PINES MARKET
Open daily in season from 9 to 7

Barney and Cheryl Barnes work their small farm the natural way. Rows of vegetables are sown in strip beds, crops are rotated to maximize the season and everything is hand picked. So fresh is the produce that if Cheryl doesn't have it in the retail shed, she'll excuse herself to go pick it for you. They raise a few chickens for farm fresh eggs, a few pigs for juicy pork, grow lots of vegetables and bring in fruit from neighbouring farms. www.inthepinesonline.com

1320 Seventh St Louth, St Catharines

The best approach to food is simple. Simply eat the best, the freshest, the healthiest and the tastiest - eat local.

leeks and mushrooms with pancetta

2 tablespoons (30 mL) Ontario canaola oil
2 slices pancetta, cut into thin strips
1 pound (.45 kg) white button mushrooms, washed and cut in half
1 leek, thinly sliced, white and pale green parts only
1 teaspoon (5 mL) fresh thyme leaves
Ontario salt

Heat the oil in a skillet over medium-low heat and cook the pancetta until almost crisp, about 5 minutes. Remove from the skillet and add the mushrooms. Cook until the mushrooms have released their water and it has all but evaporated. Add leeks and thyme, return the pancetta to the skillet and sauté until leeks are soft, about 2 minutes. Season well. Serves 4 to 6.

Perth County

ANNE SLATER'S FRESH ORGANIC VEGETABLES
Open on Saturdays in season

On 1.5 acres, Ann Slater has been growing organic specialty lettuces and other vegetables for three decades. In the beginning it was from the farm stand and then when the farmers' market opened in St. Mary's, just west of Stratford, she began to sell there and discovered just how many people wanted to buy her fresh-picked produce. This is partly because her lettuces are fresh and organic but also because they are beautiful to look at. In addition to her farm stand and the St. Mary's Farmers' Market, Community Supported Agriculture (CSA) customers receive weekly vegetable deliveries from Ann. www.ontariofarmfresh.com

157030 15th Line Zorra, Lakeside

local food in

Middlesex County

Throughout Middlesex County you'll find yellow brick farmhouses, usually trimmed with Victorian details painted in a creamy blonde to complement the brick. The homes will typically have a large arched window filled with handsome stained glass detail. These houses can also be found throughout rural Perth and Elgin Counties. It's a unique country architectural feature that is noticeably concentrated in downtown London bringing a bit of country into the city.

London is a great food city with farmers' markets and restaurants dedicated to local foods. Restaurants like Garlic's and the Black Trumpet are eateries that offer a flavour of the region. The Only on King has been recognized by enRoute magazine as an up and coming restaurant. Braise Food & Wine, adjacent to a new boutique hotel, is a more recent culinary addition to the London restaurant scene. Executive Chef Kristian Crossen is a former Langdon Hall chef who brings his local sensibilities into downtown London.

Covent Garden Farmers' Market is in the heart of downtown London. In addition to this big city market the Masonville Farmers' Market is exclusively a farmer-based market with 60 vendors at the peak of harvest season and the Western Fair Farmers' Market is moving in that direction with farmers coming from Middlesex, Elgin, Perth and Huron counties.

Middlesex is known as the 'bread basket' of Ontario with an abundance of large farms growing a variety of grains. The largest grain farmer in Ontario, Arva Heights is situated in Middlesex County and just outside the city of London in the Masonville area is a small artisan mill, Arva Flour

Mill & Store (www.arvaflourmill.com). Mike Matthews is 4th generation miller who produces spelt, hard and soft flours in both white and whole wheat varieties. The grains are milled weekly for the freshest flour available.

Middlesex is dotted with pretty little villages like Dorchester, Lucan, Glencoe, Wardsville, Parkhill and Strathroy that are worth the drive. In between you'll find Heeman's Greenhouses and Strawberry Farm, a large farm market offering sweet fruit and sweet corn throughout the season or you can pick your own vegetables from the Thomas Brothers Market and U-Pick Farm.

White Crest Mushroom Farm in just east of London and produces a variety of specialty mushrooms as well as frozen mushrooms. Marc's Mushrooms is a company run by Marc Eber, a forager who collects wild mushrooms and other edibles such as wild leeks, fiddleheads, nuts and berries. He searches for morels, black trumpet, chanterelles and hedgehog mushrooms in the forests around Ontario and sells to restaurants and the Western Fair Farmers' Market.

Spend time sipping the delicious flavours. Quai du Vin Winery, produces fine dinner wines while, Rush Creek Wines vinifies luscious fruit in season and Clover Mead makes great honey wine. Carolinian Winery on Foley Farms is both a fruit and table winery with an on-site restaurant

London-Middlesex has farmers' markets, on-farm markets that offer fresh food in season and many artisan food shops stocking local products.

London-Middlesex Local Food Guide | www.middlesextourism.ca
Middlesex London Get Fresh Eat Local | www.eatlocallondon.com

enjoy with

HUFF ESTATES WINERY
Chardonnay
www.huffestates.com

oyster mushrooms with black peanut chili sauce

2 tablespoons (30 mL) Ontario peanut oil
1 carrot, cut into thin sticks
1 field zucchini, cut into thin sticks
1/2 head fresh broccoli, cut into florets
2 scallions, finely sliced
3 cups (750 mL) oyster mushrooms
1 teaspoon (5 mL) Ontario peanut butter
3 tablespoons (45 mL) water
1/2 teaspoon (2.5 mL) dried chili flakes
2 tablespoons (30 mL) Ontario black peanuts
Ontario salt

Heat a wok over a high heat. Add the oil and heat until very hot. Toss in the carrots, zucchini, broccoli and scallions and stir fry for one minute. Add the mushrooms and cook until they have softened. Mix the peanut butter and water and add to the wok. Cook for a minute, add the chili flakes and peanuts and season well. Stir fry for another minute before serving. Serves 4 to 6.

Norfolk County

KERNAL PEANUTS
Open Monday to Friday from 9 to 5:30, Saturday from 10 and Sunday only in season.

Do you think Ernie and Nancy Racz ever thought they'd become the largest peanut grower in Canada when they switched from tobacco growing in the '70s? They certainly didn't. They have over 150 acres now planted to different varieties of peanuts like Valencia, Virginia, Redskin and Spanish. In the quaint little retail shop in Vittoria you'll find them all, including flavoured peanuts like garlic or chili pepper. The flavours of Kernal Peanuts are richer than other commercial brands with a mellow tasting skin. My favourite is their black peanut. It's elegant, tasting a bit cashew-like with a buttery flavour on the palate, a decadent almost sweet taste and a black skin that is almost tasteless. www.canadianpeanuts.com

393 Norfolk Road 58, Vittoria

enjoy with

VINELAND ESTATES WINERY
Pinot Meunier
www.vineland.com

roasted eggplant with walnuts and yogurt

3 small eggplant, stems intact and sliced lengthwise
3 tablespoons (45 mL) Ontario canola oil
1/2 onion, minced
2 garlic cloves, minced
2 tablespoons (30 mL) Ontario yogurt
1/2 cup (125 mL) orchard walnuts, chopped
3 tablespoons (45 mL) garden coriander, finely chopped
Ontario salt

Preheat oven to 350F (180C). Lay the eggplant on a baking dish in a single layer and sprinkle with canola oil, onion and garlic. Season and bake for 40 to 45 minutes. Remove from oven and lay on a platter. Season again and drizzle with yogurt, walnuts and coriander. Serve warm.

Note: If you can't find baby eggplant, ask your favourite farmer to pick them early for you.

Northumberland

LOVSHIN FAMILY FARM
Open daily from August 1 to October 31

Mark and Christine Lovshin manage a 5-acre vegetable plot on their 8-acre farm. There are unending rows upon rows of red and yellow cooking onions, four different kinds of cucumbers, a variety of squash, red beets, plenty of green and yellow beans, and 8,000 tomato plants. They plant at various times throughout the spring so their harvest is staggered and extended. All of the produce is harvested by Christine and sold from their wagon at the entrance to their farm. Next to the roadside stand is the pastureland for their lamb. They sell the whole animal and will have it custom cut at the local abattoir.

7434 Telephone Road, Cobourg

Farmers' Markets are about building local food communities, they're living examples of Ontario's edible heritage.

spinach & gouda

2 tablespoons (30 mL) country fresh butter
1 garlic clove, minced
1 shallot, minced
2 cups (500 mL) baby spinach leaves
1 cup (250 mL) Ontario gouda, shredded
Ontario salt

Preheat oven to 350F (180C). In a large skillet, melt the butter. Add garlic and shallot. Cook for 3 minutes over medium heat or until shallot is soft. Add the spinach leaves and stir to coat with the butter. Cook for 1 minute or until the spinach just begins to wilt. Remove from heat and transfer to a baking dish. Toss with shredded cheese, and salt. Bake until cheese melts, about 5 minutes. Serves 4 to 6.

Perth County

MONFORTE DAIRY
Open Wednesday to Friday 9 to 4, Saturday 10 to 4

Ruth Klahsen is a leader in Ontario cheese making, not only because of the luscious cheeses she crafts, but because of her brilliant business mind. Ruth started the first ever cheeses Community Shared Agriculture (CSA) to build the Monforte Dairy raising over $400,000 from people like me who believe, like Ruth, in a better quality food and lifestyle. Who wouldn't support great cheese! Monforte also has a market program which means they sell cheese at many different farmers' markets from Toronto to Stratford. Check the website for a farmers' market near you. www.monfortedairy.com

49 Griffith Road E, Stratford

Local food is all about the unbroken arc from garden to table that includes growing, harvesting, preparing, eating and sharing foods from the local soils.

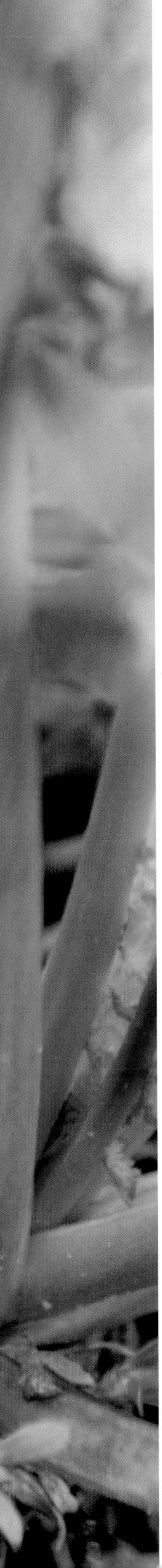

Root Vegetables: digging deep for flavour

featuring

More than 200 years ago, in 1780, Kingston became home to the first Farmers' Market in Ontario.

roasted rainbow carrots

1/2 pound (.23 kg) Ontario rainbow
carrots, peeled or unpeeled
1 tablespoon (15 mL) Ontario canola oil
2 teaspoons (10 mL) fresh thyme, chopped
2 teaspoons (10 mL) fresh chives, chopped
1 teaspoon (5 mL) Ontario extra virgin canola oil
1 teaspoon (5 mL) Niagara verjus
2 teaspoons (10 mL) Ontario honey
Ontario salt
chopped fresh thyme and chives for garnish

Preheat oven to 425F (220C). Wash and peel carrots. Lay carrots on a baking sheet and drizzle with oil. Add thyme, chives and season well. Toss well to coat and roast for about 20 to 25 minutes, depending on the size of the carrots. The skins should slightly brown and blister.

Meanwhile, in a small bowl, whisk together oil, verjus, and honey until well combined. Season well. Drizzle glaze over the cooked carrots and garnish with a sprinkling of chopped fresh thyme and chives. Serves 4 to 6.

Holland Marsh

CARRON FARMS
Wholesale or CSA program

If you've ever wondered who grows those seductive multicoloured vegetables you dream of cooking, look no further than the Verkaik family. Besides the 100 acres of onions, Jason Verkaik has 80 to 85 acres of both traditional orange and heirloom multicoloured carrots, along with colourful beets like candystriped and golden. The vegetables grow exceptionally well because of the thick, rich, jet black soils of the famous Holland Marsh. Jason is a 3rd generation LFP certified grower so he has a lot of experience to build on. Sign up for his new CSA program called Harvest Share Food Box (905-775-2432) and be one of the lucky ones to get some of these amazing vegetables throughout the season. www.carronfarms.ca

819 Canal Road, Bradford

Become a Local Food Champion by spending $10 a week on local food.

baked potato sticks

5 medium russet potatoes, scrubbed
2 tablespoons (30 mL) Ontario canola oil
coarse Ontario salt

Preheat oven to 450°F (220C). Cut the potatoes lengthwise into finger-sized slices. Toss with canola oil, and salt in a large bowl. Spread in a single layer on prepared baking sheet. Roast potato sticks until tender and brown around some edges, turning occasionally, about 35 minutes. Sprinkle with salt. Serves 4 to 6.

Frontenac County

ELM TREE FARM
Open Friday afternoon and Saturday mornings, otherwise call ahead 613-335-3361

Tom Waller and Allaine Nordin purchased their 87-acre dream farm in 1995 because they wanted to grow their own food; they believe in organic farming and have gone as far as biodynamic farming. Then like all good things, it got out of hand with friends and family wanting more and more of their amazing, delicious produce. Seven different gardens, each with their own character, equals 5 acres of vegetables under organic production that service more than 60 customers in one of Ottawa's longest running CSAs. They raise and sell frozen whole chickens, some turkeys and offer farm fresh eggs. Demeter Biodynamic certified. www.elmtreefarm.ca

1090 Hayes Road, Arden

Meet a new farmer each week and before long you will have built your very own local food community.

beet chips

2 candy cane beets
2 yellow beets
2 tablespoons (30 mL) Ontario canola oil
Ontario salt

Preheat oven to 350F (180C). Peel beets and slice thinly on a mandolin. In a large bowl, toss beets with canola oil and salt.

On two baking sheets, arrange beets in a single layer. Bake until edges of beets begin to dry out, about 20 minutes. Rotate baking sheets. Bake 10 to 20 minutes, removing chips as they become lighter in colour. Transfer to a wire rack; chips will crisp up as they cool. Serves 4.

Lanark County

QUEEN BEET FARM
Open seasonally, call ahead, 613-264-2499

Coral Sproule worked at one of Canada's largest CSA farms, Plan B Organics, before returning to her family's 98-acre farm in Bathurst. On the farm, Coral and partner, Dawson Willsey have a special interest in growing heirloom vegetables as well as raising goats and chickens. Coral sells a wide variety of delicious heirloom produce such as beets, rhubarb, different salad greens, garlic, carrots, tomatoes, melons and, of course, farm fresh eggs. You can buy from Coral right off the farm, at the Perth Farmers' Market and through her CSA program.

1026 6th Concession, Bathurst, Perth

Prince Edward County

HAGERMAN FARMS
Roadside market open seasonally from June to November

Lyle Hagerman has lived on his 550-acre farm his entire life. He grows a wide variety of vegetables not only for his market but for the Waring House & Cooking School, just down the road. Lyle makes frequent visits to the Waring House to keep close inventory on their produce and makes sure they're well stocked. Tomatoes and potatoes are his biggest seller. Lyle grows over 13 different varieties of potatoes from red skins to yellow flesh, from baking potatoes to new potatoes. Just ask Lyle what the best potato is for scalloped potatoes and he'll tell you it's Chieftan (red skin and white flesh).

13644 Loyalist Parkway, Picton

scalloped potatoes

2 pounds (.90 kg) white field potatoes,
sliced (about 6 potatoes)
6 slices country bacon, diced
2 tablespoons (30 mL) country fresh butter
1 onion, diced
3 garlic cloves
2 tablespoons (30 mL) fresh thyme
1 cup (250 mL) light cream
1 small wheel Ontario brie-style cheese, cut into slices
Ontario salt

Preheat oven to 350F (180C). Place the sliced potatoes in a large saucepan and cover with cold salted water. Cook over high heat until water is boiling. Boil for 2 minutes, remove from heat and drain. Allow to steam dry.

In a small skillet, cook bacon until crispy, about 5 minutes. Drain on paper towels. Meanwhile, melt the butter in a small saucepan over medium heat. Add onions, garlic and thyme and cook, stirring, for a few minutes until onions are soft but not browned. Warm cream in a small saucepan for 2 minutes or until warmed thoroughly. Set aside.

Layer one third of the potatoes in a greased 8-inch oven-proof casserole dish. Season well and spread half the onions and bacon over top. Repeat layers. Finish with remaining potatoes. Pour warm cream over top, using the tip of a knife to ease sauce between layers if necessary.

Place the baking dish on a baking sheet to catch the cream if it bubbles over. Cover and bake for 1 hour. Uncover and lay slices of brie on top and bake until cheese has melted and potatoes are lightly browned and tender, about 30 minutes longer. Let stand for 5 minutes before serving.

A favourite get-away for many Ontarians.

local food in

Huron County

Huron County is quintessential farm country on the east shore of its namesake, Lake Huron. This farmland, with plenty of corn, wheat and soy, is a favourite get-away for many Ontarians.

Jon and I took a liking to Goderich, a destination with everything you'd expect in a port town and then some. Large lake steamers crest the horizon and there's evidence of the dredging activities of Sifto Salt, but there's also sophisticated recreation along the sandy beaches and the beautiful 1.5 km long beach front boardwalk. Take an evening stroll along the never ending boardwalk and you'll see some of the most beautiful sunsets in the province.

There's a small kiosk on the dock by the Sifto Salt mine that fries up some of the freshest fish around. I was enjoying my perch and chips on a nearby sandy picnic table when a seagull scooped it up with lightning speed – what fun! The town has a culinary charm with kitchen stores, some which offer cooking classes.

Travelling inland, the horizon is dotted with silos. This is Hensall, the white bean capital of Canada and the silos hold thousands of tons. A local brand name for dried beans is Thompson's and you'll find them on grocery shelves. I'm told what Thompson's doesn't use in their packages of dried beans, Unico, in Essex County, puts into tins.

Hensall is also known as the home of The Garlic Box. They source fresh garlic in season from across the province and turn it into delicious and creative food products. Look for them in specialty food shops.

The Benmiller Inn is in nearby Benmiller, and Executive Chef Jeffrey Hicks likes to surround himself with local foods. When Jon and I stopped in for lunch, we noticed a group of farmers being treated to lunch from the produce they'd delivered. This is local food at its best!

A friend and I had dinner at the romantic Little Inn at Bayfield; they prepared a cassoulet from local ingredients. It was beyond amazing – savoury with white beans simmered with smoked meats and rich herbs.

Jon and I regard Bayfield as a great culinary destination. For a small village, it offers world class accommodation, boutique shopping along the historic street and wonderful local food shops. Stop in for lunch at the Black Dog Pub, owned and operated by cookbook author and culinary guru, Kathleen Sloan-McIntosh and her husband Ted. Check out their cooking classes, Kathleen always serves up scrumptious fun.

Huron County has a local food web directory, agriculture and culinary map, 6 farmers' markets and lots of markets on farms that offer fresh food in season.

Huron Perth Farm to Table | www.huronperthfarmtotable.ca

Taste of Huron County | www.tasteofhuron.ca

Thunder Bay

BELLUZ FARM
Open weekends from spring to end of October, 11 to 5

Don, Claire, Kevin, Jodi and Lily Belluz want to do their bit for the environment so they encourage the use of cloth bags by declaring their farm a plastic bag-free zone. You can pick your own fruit and vegetables or buy them ready picked for you. Belluz is a fantastic farm in the beautiful Slate River Valley. Besides seasonal produce, you'll find maple syrup, local meats and cheeses in their on-site farmers' market. There's also a Harvest Café that features fresh local food. A great corn maze, wagon rides and great fresh country air attract thousands to Belluz Farms. www.locallygrown.net | www.belluzfarms.on.ca

752 Candy Mountain Drive, Thunder Bay

candy cane beets

20 baby candy cane beets, unpeeled, washed
4 fresh cut rosemary sprigs
2 tablespoons (30 mL) country fresh butter
1/4 cup (60 mL) Ontario extra virgin canola oil
2 spring onions, sliced
Ontario salt
rosemary sprigs as garnish

Preheat oven to 375F (190C). Place beets in roasting pan just large enough to hold the beets. Add rosemary sprigs and enough water to barely cover beets. Cover pan tightly with foil. Roast beets until tender, about an hour. Remove from oven and cool completely. Transfer beets to work surface. Peel and quarter. You can roast beets the evening before you want to serve them.

When ready to serve, preheat oven to 350°F (180C). Melt butter with oil in small saucepan. Pour over beets in the roasting pan with onions. Season well and toss to coat. Bake until heated through, stirring occasionally, about 20 minutes. Transfer to bowl. Garnish with additional rosemary sprigs. Serves 4 to 6.

Always play music in your kitchen and invite friends over to help with a meal. Good food demands to be shared.

roasted root vegetables

4 carrots, peeled and cut in half lengthwise
1 tablespoon (15 mL) Ontario apple cider vinegar
1 tablespoon (15 mL) extra virgin canola oil
1 sprig of rosemary, minced
1 fennel bulb, outer layer discarded, quartered
1 tablespoon (15 mL) Niagara verjus
1 tablespoon (15 mL) extra virgin canola oil
parsley leaves, torn
4 parsnips, peeled and cut in half lengthwise
1 tablespoon (15 mL) Ontario white wine vinegar
1 tablespoon (15 mL) extra virgin canola oil
8 sage leaves, torn
4 beets, quartered
1 tablespoon (15 mL) Ontario balsamic vinegar
1 tablespoon (15 mL) extra virgin canola oil
2 bay leaves
4 turnips, quartered
1 tablespoon (15 mL) Ontario red wine vinegar
1 tablespoon (15 mL) extra virgin canola oil
1 teaspoon (5 mL) fresh thyme leaves
Ontario salt

Prepare the vegetables and parboil them separately in salted water for 5 to 7 minutes until al dente. Cook the beets last as they'll take about 25 to 30 minutes. Put the carrots in a bowl and add cider vinegar, oil and rosemary and season generously. Toss and when cool, put them in a bag to marinate. Put the fennel in a bowl and add verjus, oil, parsley and season. Toss and when cool, put them in a bag to marinate. Put the parsnips in a bowl and add white wine vinegar, oil, sage and season. Toss and when cool, put them in a bag to marinate. Put the beets in a bowl and add balsamic vinegar, oil, bay leaves and season. Toss marinate in a bag when cool. Put the turnips in a bowl and add red wine vinegar, oil, thyme and season. Toss and marinate in a bag when cool. Refrigerate vegetables overnight.

When ready to cook, preheat oven to 375F (190C). Remove the vegetables from their bags and lay them in a roasting pan. Roast the vegetables for 50 minutes to 1 hour until they are golden and crispy. Serves 4 to 6.

Wellington-Guelph

100-MILE MARKET
Local food delivery service

This market is the link between grower and restaurateur, grocer, specialty food shop and consumer. The company was started in 2007 by Albert Knab, Chris McKittrick and Paul Knechtel because Knab, who farms 100 acres was frustrated in his search for viable, sustainable local food delivery options for his produce. 100-Mile Markets has a growing number of over 160 Ontario farmers and producers who grow, raise and process an amazing choice of local meats, fish, vegetables, fruit, dairy, grains, legumes, oils, vinegars, mustards and preserves. They sell, market and distribute local food year-round. Consumers can order from the website and pick up their order in either Kitchener-Waterloo or Burlington. www.100milemarket.com

235 Ardelt Avenue, Kitchener

CRANAPPLE CIDER
CRANAPPLE CIDER
CRANAPPLE CIDER
APPLE CIDER

skillet potatoes, onions and garlic

3 tablespoons (45 mL) Ontario vegetable oil
1/2 pound (.23 kg) red skin potatoes
1/2 pound (.23 kg) blue potatoes
1/2 pound (.23 kg) yellow flesh potatoes
3 small onions, sliced
8 cloves garlic, peeled
Ontario salt
1 tablespoon (15 mL) fresh garden thyme, chopped
2 to 4 thyme sprigs

Heat the oil in a large sauté pan until quite hot. Add the potatoes, onions, and garlic all at once, stirring to coat. Season with salt and add the thyme sprigs. Reduce the heat to medium and cook uncovered, stirring occasionally, until the onions are soft and the potatoes are tender and golden, about 30 minutes. Season again and serve.

Muskoka

BROOKLANDS FARM
Open Monday through Saturday, May to October

I find it absolutely amazing that Katya and Ken Riley can grow the variety of vegetables and berries that they do from their 300-acre farm. It's easy to see how much they love the land and the lifestyle it provides them. They're eager to host cooking classes and other workshops related to sustainable living in their new culinary studio which was renovated from the original log homestead on the farm. The beautiful century barn provides a stunning site for country weddings and events. the 30 acres of gardens produce 30 different types of potatoes, Jeusalem artichokes, 5 different types of gourmet beans, garlic, sweet corn, strawberries, raspberries and as Katya puts it, "anything that we can grow in Muskoka, we do."
www.brooklandsfarm.ca | www.savourmuskoka.com

1375 Butter and Egg Road, Milford Bay

This book is dedicated to the amazing farmers who labour long for foodies like me.

sweet potatoes with walnuts and balsamic

4 cups (1 L) sweet potatoes, peeled and diced
3 tablespoons (45 mL) Ontario vegetable oil
1 teaspoon (5 mL) dried thyme leaves
1 onion, sliced
1 clove garlic, sliced
1/2 cup (125 mL) whole orchard walnuts
1 tablespoon (15 mL) Ontario balsamic vinegar
Ontario salt

Preheat oven to 425F (220C). In large bowl combine the potatoes, oil and thyme. Season well. Mix well to coat the potatoes. Pour into a baking pan and cook for 20 minutes. Remove from oven, stir, baste and add onions and garlic. Bake for another 15 minutes. Remove from oven, stir, baste and add walnuts. Bake for an additional 6 minutes. To serve, drizzle with balsamic vinegar and season. Serves 4 to 6.

Norfolk County

SOVEREIGN FARM
On-farm market open daily from May to September, 10 to 6

Wes Sovereign's parents were market gardeners and he has fond memories of helping them to sell the produce at the farmers' market. In 1993 Wes and Brenda bought a 29-acre farm and a short 2 years later, happily became full time farmers. In the summer, their market vegetable garden swells to 10 acres with an abundance of produce that they sell at the St Lawrence Farmers' Market, the Metro Hall Farmers' Market and the Ancaster Farmers' Market. They have an entire acre dedicated to greenhouse production for tomatoes, from cherry to yellow, roma and more. www.sovereignfarms.ca

130 Lutesville Road, Waterford

local food in

Waterloo County

This region, made famous by its Oktoberfest celebrations, is much more than the popular beer party could ever suggest.

ST. JACOBS

At the heart of Waterloo's culinary culture is the much loved St. Jacobs Farmers' Market that draws foodies province-wide. In the large buildings meat and dairy are sold while the outside stalls hold vegetables of all kinds, from bushels of multi-coloured beets to sacks of potatoes, cups of interesting mushrooms to pints of tiny tomatoes so sweet I eat them like candy while I walk around soaking up the sights, sounds and smells of a bustling country farmers' market.

FARMERS' MARKET

Another jewel of the region is the Kitchener Farmers' Market. It's open year-round, and while it may be one of the oldest farmers' markets in the province, it's also one of the more progressive, offering cooking classes that feature different and delicious ways to use and preserve fresh-from-the-farm produce. Here, the vegetables are complemented with artisan cheese, organic foods and baked goods.

Meat is big at this country market, especially fresh and cured sausages. Jon and I came across a vendor who makes 12 different kinds of pepperettes with heat levels that range from 'mild' all the way up to 'worse than suicide'! There are stalls that offer baked goods and preserves, honey and small farm implements. It's definitely worth the trip whether you're a serious cook or simply want to devour the sights of the best food the seasons have to offer.

MENNONITE COUNTRY

It's worth driving the back roads into the beautiful rolling hills where you'll find farm stands at the end of most farm laneways. Waterloo County is Mennonite country, so don't be surprised to find horse and buggies driving the roads. Jon and I drove around the county on a Sunday morning, looking for the church with its horse and buggy parking lot. What fun!

The Elmira Fruit and Vegetable Auction is a genuine auction, owned and run by a group of Mennonite farmers. Established in 2004, it supports local growers by allowing them to bring their produce to the auction for sale. Each week the produce available is different, and wholesale lots range from pallets and field bins to as small as half a bushel or bag.

BUTTER TART TRAIL

Just a little north of this region I found a delicious Butter Tart Trail. I have to admit, I don't know anyone that doesn't have a soft spot for Ontario butter tarts of all kinds – from raisins to nuts or runny to firm.

From that moment, I made it my quest to taste all of the butter tarts I found in Ontario. I have to say I've found devilishly delicious examples at farm markets, farmers' markets and small town bakeries. Check out the trail at www.wellington-north.com/whats-on/butter-tart-trail.aspx. Along this route, you'll find more than a dozen different varieties to tempt you.

Waterloo has a local food web directory, agriculture and culinary map, farmers' markets and lots of markets on farms that offer fresh food in season.

Food Link Waterloo | www.foodlink.ca
Explore Waterloo | www.explorewaterlooregion.ca

It is possible to buy local all year round. Like the seasons, the foods will change from freshly harvested lettuce greens to root vegetables. Foods available year round include bread and pastries, cheese, meat, flour, juice, jam, vinegar, breads and wine.

The Bread Box

featuring

Ontario

ONTARIO FARM FRESH

This provincial organization helps on-farm markets promote themselves. There are hundreds of on-farm markets tucked snugly among the orchards, gardens, fields, vineyards and backroads of Ontario. Some are as small as a wagon parked road-side. Others are completely restored barns that offer venues for weddings, theatre and parties. Large or small, they all offer quintessential farm and country conviviality that is wholesome and nurturing to young and old alike. Visit an on-farm market with the family and enjoy wagon rides and corn mazes. Buy some just-picked garden vegetables or fresh country meats, a freshly baked pie or jar of wildflower honey. Pick your own strawberries, pumpkins, apples - even Christmas trees! Warm up to a steamy mug of cider or a boiled ear of buttery corn. Meet the farmer and learn about your food; you'll find a farm near you at www.ontariofarmfresh.com

apple cider muffins

1/2 cup (125 mL) country fresh butter, room temperature
3/4 cup (180 mL) brown sugar
1 farm fresh egg
1 1/2 cups (375 mL) all-purpose flour
1 teaspoon (5 mL) baking powder
1/2 teaspoon (2.5 mL) baking soda
pinch of salt
3/4 cup (180 mL) Ontario apple cider
2 farm fresh egg whites
pinch of Ontario salt
4 tablespoons (60 mL) water
1/2 cup (125 mL) dark brown sugar
3 tablespoons (45 mL) Kittling Ridge 40
Creek Whisky (optional)
1/2 cup (125 mL) farm fresh butter, room temperature
Ontario apple slices for garnish

Preheat oven to 350F (180C). In the bowl of an electric mixer cream the butter and brown sugar until light and fluffy, about 3 minutes. Add the egg and beat until well incorporated.

Meanwhile, in another bowl, whisk the flour, baking powder, baking soda and salt together. Add to the butter cream mixture alternately with apple cider. Beat on medium speed until ingredients are just combined.

Scoop the batter into 12 muffin cups and bake for 30 minutes or until muffins are beginning to brown around the edges. Completely cool before icing.

Whip the egg whites with salt until soft peaks form. Put the water and brown sugar in a saucepan and bring to a boil. Boil for approximately 3 minutes. Remove the brown sugar syrup from heat and slowly drizzle into the egg whites while the whisk is running on medium speed. Drizzle until half the syrup is used. Add the whisky (optional). Add butter and continue to whisk, but do not over whisk or it will begin to curdle. Chill frosting before topping the muffins. Garnish with slices of Ontario apple. Makes 12 muffins.

Wellington-Guelph

MAPLETON ORGANIC DAIRY

Open daily with summer and winter hours Ineke Booy and Martin de Groot ran their 250-acre farm conventionally yet they couldn't shake the growing concern their actions had on the environment, their health, the community and the welfare of their animals. They didn't want to be commodity producers, but rather food producers. They decided to go organic and today the farm consists of 600 acres of certified organic land, 75 milking cows and their offspring. Mapleton's Organic Dairy was born in 1999, when they began processing milk into organic ice cream, frozen yogurt, and fresh yogurt. You can buy their organic products and more at their on-farm retail store and café. www.mapletonsorganic.ca

8548 Wellington Road 7, Drayton

black plum yogurt loaf

2 tablespoons (30 mL) cabernet ice syrup
1 1/2 cups (375 mL) black plums, pitted and diced
6 tablespoons (90 mL) country fresh
butter, room temperature
3/4 cup (180 mL) sugar
3 farm fresh eggs
1 1/2 cups (375 mL) all-purpose flour
2 teaspoons (10 mL) baking powder
3/4 cup (180 mL) plain creamy yogurt

Preheat oven to 350F (180C). In a medium bowl, pour the ice syrup over the plums. Mix well and set aside to marinate. In an electric mixer, cream the butter and sugar for about 2 minutes on medium speed. Add the eggs one at a time, incorporating well after each one. In a separate bowl, whisk the flour and baking powder together and add to the butter mixture alternately with the yogurt until both are incorporated; careful not to over mix.

Meanwhile, drain the plums. Pour the batter into a loaf pan and smooth the top. Press the plums into the batter and bake for 55 to 60 minutes or until golden brown and a toothpick inserted in the centre comes out clean. Serve hot or cold as desired.

cheddar cheese puffs

1 1/2 cups (375 mL) whole milk
1/2 cup (125 mL) country fresh butter
1 tablespoon (15 mL) Ontario salt
1 teaspoon (5 mL) freshly ground black pepper
1 1/2 cups (375 mL) all-purpose flour
5 farm fresh eggs
1 cup (250 mL) Ontario aged cheddar cheese, shredded
1/2 cup (125 mL) Ontario parmesan cheese, grated
1/4 cup (60 mL) Ontario aged cheddar cheese, shredded

Heat oven to 375F (190C). Line 2 baking sheets with parchment paper.

Combine milk, butter, salt and pepper in a medium saucepan and bring to a boil over medium heat. Reduce heat to low, add flour all at once, and stir vigorously until well incorporated. Cook, stirring constantly, until dough feels dry to the touch and is no longer sticking to the bottom of the pan, about 2 to 3 minutes.

Transfer dough to a mixer fitted with a paddle attachment. Beat in eggs one at a time on medium-low speed, letting the first one completely incorporate before adding the next. Add cheddar and parmesan cheeses to the dough and mix on low until incorporated.

Drop tablespoon-size rounds of dough on the prepared baking sheets, about 1/2 inch apart. Evenly sprinkle cheddar cheese over puffs and give another grinding of black pepper. Bake until puffed and golden brown, about 30 to 35 minutes. Serve hot, warm, or at room temperature. Makes 2 dozen puffs.

Hamilton-Wentworth

PARON CHEESE
Open Monday through Saturday, 9 to 5

This may be one of Ontario's oldest artisan cheese companies. The Paron family emigrated from Italy in 1931 and today remains the only artisan cheese company allowed to age classic Italian-style cheeses on the traditional ageworn wooden boards. Run by Myrna Paron and her daughter Natalie, Paron Cheese crafts artisan-style parmesan (also available grated), a pecorino-style goat cheese, Casata, mozzarella, Friulano and cheddar. Montasio, their flagship cheese is creamy and buttery when young and nutty; earthy and firmer when aged. When old, it grates beautifully and can be used instead of parmesan in any recipe. You can buy direct from the cheese factory.

400 Hwy 20, Binbrook

corn fritters

1 1/3 cup (325 mL) all-purpose flour
2 teaspoons (10 mL) baking powder
pinch of Ontario salt
1 farm fresh egg, beaten
3/4 cup (180 mL) milk
1 1/2 cups (375 mL) fresh corn kernels
2 spring onions, diced
Ontario canola oil

In a mixing bowl, whisk the flour, baking powder and salt together. Beat egg in a small bowl until frothy. Add egg and milk to flour mixture. Stir gently until mixed. A few lumps are still ok. Add corn and onions and mix to incorporate well.

Heat about 4 inches of vegetable oil in a large pot. Drop tablespoons of fritter batter into the hot oil, leaving enough room for each to move around. Turn over when bottom is golden and cook until golden. Drain on paper towels. Makes approximately 24 corn fritters.

Wellington Guelph

STROM'S
Open daily 10 to 6

In the winter of 2002 Channing Strom and his kids designed a giant corn maze. The very next spring they decided to map it out on 60 acres of land for a total of 3 miles of maze fun. Today, the Stroms are famous for creating unique and intricate mazes on the land and donating all of the proceeds to charity. It's a great farm and country tradition for an entire community. The Stroms sell over 144,000 ears of corn each year. They pick only one ear per stalk and they're picked in small batches continually. In the on-site market, the time of picking will be displayed so you know your corn is just hours fresh. They also sell fresh baked goods and frozen corn.
www.strom.ca | www.ontariofarmfresh.ca

5089 Wellington Road, Guelph

Perth County has a local food web directory, agriculture and culinary map, farmers' markets and lots of markets on farms that offer fresh food in season.

Visit Perth | www.visitperth.ca
Welcome to Stratford | www.welcometostratford.com
Savour Statford | www.welcometostratford.com

local food in

Perth County

Steeped in culture and theatre, the town of Stratford is the centre of agriculturally rich Perth County. I would never have coupled farming and theatre, but it works beautifully when you add hospitality to the mix. This is also the home of one of Ontario's most prestigious culinary schools: The Stratford Chefs School.

SAVOUR STRATFORD

It's definitely a cultural, culinary and entertainment pocket tucked neatly into vast stretches of farmland. Home to some of the most innovative and dramatic (must be the theatre influence!) farmers you'll meet. In fact, you have a chance to meet them at the annual culinary festival, Savour Stratford Perth County (each September). I think it's one of the best local food culinary festivals around.

CULINARY SCHOOL

Paul Finkelstein is a chef/instructor at Northwestern Secondary School. Here, he teaches culinary skills in a classroom that has spread outside to vegetable gardens. Paul opened a cafeteria at the school called the Screaming Avocado. It focuses totally on local food. The cafeteria and monthly local food dinners the class holds for the community, allows them to travel to learn more about food. The last time I spoke to Paul, his high school class had just returned from touring British Columbia farms and they were smoking ricotta. He also mentioned something about getting a cow – sounds nothing like my high school but Paul is serious about ingraining young minds with the importance of local food.

The back roads are filled with pork and dairy farms. Stratford has a community project that collects vegetable scraps from many of the restaurants and delivers them to Perth Pork Products for the pigs to eat. The resulting pork is in huge demand from the high-end Stratford restaurateurs.

CHEESE

Monforte Dairy has an innovative financial structure where the public gets to directly support its delicious initiatives. I'm proud to say Jon and I signed up and we were paid back in cheese – lots and lots of the most amazingly delicious and exciting cheese – can you imagine a better payback?

QUAINT TOWNS

This region has many small quaint towns and villages waiting to be discovered. If you're one of the thousands who drive right by St. Marys on your way to Stratford, you're not alone. A quintessential farm town with the beautiful Thames River winding through it, the grounds are manicured to perfection and buildings beautifully renovated. Here you'll find the last original train station, restored true to its heritage and architecturally beautiful. It's also home to C'est Bon Cheese, and any town with its own fromagerie has to be pretty good!

Perth County is a patchwork of fields of soybeans, feed corn and wheat. Rolling hills are dotted with sprawling farm estates, characterized by big red barns, tall silos and yellow brick farm houses. The yellow brick was once made in local brickyards and the region is distinguished by typical honey-coloured Victorian homes.

enjoy with
ZIRALDO
Vidal Icewine
www.ziraldo.ca

blueberry brioche

1 envelope quick rise dry active yeast
3 tablespoons (45 mL) warm water
1/2 teaspoon (2.5 mL) Ontario salt
1 tablespoon (15 mL) sugar
2 cups (500 mL) all-purpose flour
3 farm fresh eggs, lightly beaten
1/3 cup (80 mL) country fresh butter, room temperature
1 egg yolk
milk for wash
1 cup (250 mL) just-picked blueberries
1 tablespoon (15 mL) fruit sugar
2 tablespoons (30 mL) Niagara verjus
1 teaspoon (5 mL) fresh mint, minced
mint sprigs for garnish

Stir the yeast into the water with the salt and sugar. Set aside for five minutes to dissolve. Put the flour in the bowl of an electric mixer and use the dough hook attachment. Add the eggs and the yeast and mix it slowly to make a soft, sticky dough. Work in the butter a piece at a time to create a smooth, sticky dough.

Shape the dough in the brioche tins. Set it in a warm spot and let it rise for 2 hours. Preheat the oven to 425F (220C). Whisk the egg yolk and milk together, glaze the brioche and bake for 25 to 30 minutes. Makes 10 individual loaves.

To make the blueberry compote, put the blueberries, fruit sugar, verjus and fresh mint in a small saucepan pan over medium heat. Cook until the blueberries are warmed through, about 2 minutes, then simmer for 2 to 3 minutes more. Some of the blueberries will pop, releasing their juices.

To serve, cut the tops off 6 brioche. Carve out a cavity in each one and fill with warm blueberries. Garnish with a sprig of mint and place top on blueberries. Serve warm or chilled.

Essex County

KLASSEN BLUEBERRIES
Open 9 to 8 daily from mid July to mid September

You can't miss it; clouds of blue nets hover over 35 acres of lush blueberry bushes on County Road 50 between Kingsville and Colchester in Essex County. Ted and Celia Klassen produce over 150,000 pounds of large, juicy black pearls annually. Blueberry aficionados will pick their own while others thirsty for local food come by to buy by the pound. The Klassens have a bake shop and ice cream bar on site where you can buy a freshly baked blueberry pie or blueberry sundae. It's no surprise to discover Celia has developed her own recipe for an amazing blueberry sauce. www.klassenblueberries.com

954 County Road 50 East, Blueberry hotline, 519-738-4089

enjoy with

ARCHIBALD ORCHARDS & ESTATE WINERY
McIntosh
www.archibaldswinery.com

egg toast with maple caramelized apples

4 tablespoons (60 mL) country fresh butter
1 cup (250 mL) sugar
1 tablespoon (15 mL) Ontario maple syrup
3 large Spy apples, peeled, cored and sliced
2 farm fresh eggs
1/4 cup (60 mL) whole milk
1 teaspoon (5 mL) pure vanilla extract
6 1-inch thick slices egg bread
butter for frying
1 recipe caramel ice cream, Page 296

Heat oven to 450F (230 C). In a skillet, add butter, sugar and maple syrup. Cook over medium heat, shaking the pan occasionally (don't stir), until the sugar melts into the butter and the mixture bubbles. Continue for another 5 minutes. Meanwhile, add the apples to an 8x10-inch baking dish and pour maple sauce over top. Bake for 30 minutes or until the apples give up their liquid and it evaporates and the sides of the mass are dark brown and sticky looking. This could be considerably longer depending on the water content of your apples. Remove from oven and let cool.

Meanwhile, in a shallow mixing bowl whisk together the eggs, milk and vanilla. Quickly dip slices of egg bread in egg mixture, careful not to let it soak up too much. Place egg-soaked bread in an ovenproof skillet with butter and cook over medium heat until slightly browned on both sides but not cooked through. Transfer egg bread to the oven for the last 10 minutes of the maple apple baking time. Remove both from oven and serve hot with caramel ice cream. Serves 6.

Leeds & Grenville

KILMARNOCK ORCHARDS
On-farm market open daily in season

It doesn't get any fresher than buying from a farm market. Myriam Belot Edwards believes this is true for the produce as well as the experiences. Visit the farm where she grows 25 varieties of apples, vegetables and herbs from the orchards and gardens. She offers pick-your-own experiences, wagon rides, farm tours, cider-pressing demonstrations and picnic tables. There's a bakery in the Apple Shoppe for some fresh baked apple pies and lots of baked apple pastries that go so well with a jug of cider. The farm is tucked on the beautiful little island of Kilmarnock overlooking the Rideau River. www.kilmarnockorchard.ca

1182 Kilmarnock Road, Jasper

grape and rosemary foccacia

1 1/2 cups (375 mL) all-purpose flour
1/4 cup (60 mL) sugar
1 package instant yeast
pinch of Ontario salt
1/3 cup (80 mL) warm water
2 tablespoons (30 mL) Ontario canola oil
1 cup (250 mL) Coronation Sovereign black seedless grapes
3 sprigs garden fresh rosemary, leaves picked
Fifth Town chevre cheese

Mix the flour, sugar, yeast and salt in a bowl. Add water and canola oil and mix with a wooden spoon. Shape the dough into a ball, then knead for 10 minutes on a floured surface. Roll the dough into a circle 3/4-inch thick and transfer to an oiled baking sheet. Cover loosely with plastic wrap and leave in a warm place to rise for 20 minutes, until puffed.

Preheat the oven to 350F (180C). Form indentations in the dough with your fingertips and push in the grapes. Scatter over the rosemary and plenty of coarse salt. Bake on the top shelf of the oven. After 20 minutes, remove from the baking sheet and place the loaf directly onto the oven shelf, to allow the bottom to brown. After another 5 minutes, remove from the oven and allow to cool before serving. Serve with plenty of chevre.

Prince Edward County

FIFTH TOWN ARTISAN CHEESE CO
Open daily, check the summer and winter hours on the web

This little fromagerie makes exceptional goat and sheep milk cheeses in Prince Edward County or, as the locals call it, 'The County'. Owner Petra Cooper insists on the highest quality, which is why she only works with LFP (Local Food Plus) certified growers and insists everything they do to produce cheese is of the highest quality. Just visit them and you'll see for yourself how impressive a fromagerie can be with a bit of respect for the environment and people. In their retail shop you'll find both pasteurized and raw milk cheeses such as the delicious chevre, feta, ricotta and other hard and soft cheeses. The retail store and cheese factory have achieved Platinum LEED certification, the highest level possible.
www.fifthtown.ca | www.tastethecounty.ca

4309 County Road 8, Picton

harvest loaf

2 tablespoons (30 mL) Ontario canola oil
2 garlic cloves, roughly chopped
1/4 cup (60 mL) shallots, minced
6 button mushrooms, washed and sliced
1 jalapeno pepper, seeded and diced
1/2 cup (125 mL) field zucchini, chopped
1/2 red pepper, chopped
3 tablespoons (45 mL) fresh garden herbs such
as basil, parsley, chives or oregano
2 farm fresh eggs
1/3 cup (80 mL) whipping cream
2/3 cup (160 mL) milk
1 teaspoon (5 mL) Ontario salt
1 tablespoon (15 mL) baking powder
1 3/4 cup (430 mL) all purpose flour

Warm canola oil in a skillet over medium heat. Add garlic and shallots and cook until shallots are soft. Add the mushrooms and cook until the mushrooms give off their liquid. Add the jalapeno, zucchini, red pepper and herbs. Season and cook until the vegetables begin to soften, about 3 minutes. Set aside.

Preheat oven to 350F (180C). Wipe a loaf pan with oil and set aside. Beat the eggs with the cream and milk until well incorporated. Whisk the salt, baking powder and flour together and add to the egg mixture. Do not over mix. Fold almost all of the cooled vegetables into the dough and pour into a prepared loaf pan. Put the remaining vegetables on the top of the loaf and bake for 50 minutes. Remove from oven and place the pan on a baking rack. When cool enough to handle, remove the harvest loaf from the pan and allow to cool completely on the baking rack. Makes 1 loaf.

Waterloo County

HERRLE'S COUNTRY FARM MARKET
Open daily from mid June to end of October

Howard and Elsie Herrle started a little market in Waterloo in 1964. Their children Karen, James and Michelle, and Joanne and Trevor are second generation Herrles to run the farm and market that is now composed of 4 farms and over 450 acres of land. A whopping 250 acres are dedicated to vegetable production. They grow everything including peas, beans, sweet corn, spinach, zucchini and tomatoes and what they don't grow, they source from local farmers in the area. In the market you'll notice little shopping bag-shaped signs that tell you where the food comes from and how far. There's also an on-site bakery where they make their own baked goods using much of their own vegetables and fruit. They also make a line of preserves and their pickled sugar snap peas have become famous. www.herrles.com

1243 Erb's Road, St Agatha

Oxford County

JAKEMAN'S MAPLE SYRUP
Open Monday to Saturday 10 to 4, closed on Sundays except in the month of March

In a blind tasting of 8 maple syrups sponsored by the National Post, Jakeman's Maple Syrup came out as number one! Mary and Bob Jakeman are 4th generation maple syrup farmers who were taught the skill of making maple syrup from the aboriginal people who lived down the road. The secret techniques are passed down from one generation to another through the Jakeman men. "I don't know what it is," laughs Mary. They've just come out with a delicious new product that is a blend of maple syrup and icewine. The flavour is a sophisticated layering of butter over butterscotch with luscious toasty, honey flavours with an essence of peach and none of the fierceness one associates with sweet honey. Definitely not as sweet as maple syrup or icewine. You can buy different grades of maple syrup and maple syrup products from their retail shop. www.themaplestore.com

454414 Trillium Line, Beachville

maple sticky buns

1 teaspoon (5 mL) sugar
1 package active dry yeast
1/2 cup (125 mL) warm water
1/2 cup (125 mL) milk
1/4 cup (60 mL) sugar
1/4 cup (60 mL) country fresh butter
1 teaspoon (5 mL) Ontario salt
4 cups (1 L) all-purpose flour
2 farm fresh eggs, beaten
3/4 cup (180 mL) country fresh butter
1/2 cup (125 mL) brown sugar
1/4 cup (60 mL) pure Ontario maple syrup
1/3 cup (80 mL) Northern pecans, chopped
3/4 cup (180 mL) brown sugar
1/3 cup (80 mL) Northern pecans, chopped
1 tablespoon (15 mL) ground cinnamon
2 tablespoons (30 mL) country fresh butter, melted

In a small bowl, dissolve sugar and yeast in warm water. Let stand until frothy, about 10 minutes. Warm the milk in a small saucepan until it bubbles, then remove from heat. Mix in sugar, butter and salt; stir until melted. Let cool until lukewarm.

Whisk the flour in a large bowl and make a well in the centre. Combine the yeast mixture, lukewarm milk and eggs, stir well to combine. Add to the flour and work together until the dough comes together, then turn it out onto a lightly-floured surface and knead until smooth and elastic, about 8 minutes. Let it rest on the counter for 5 minutes.

While dough is resting, melt butter in a small saucepan over medium heat. Stir in brown sugar and maple syrup, whisking until smooth. Pour into greased 9x13-inch baking pan. Sprinkle bottom of pan with 1/2 the pecans; set aside.

Combine brown sugar, pecans, and cinnamon; set aside.

Turn dough out onto a lightly floured surface, roll into an 18x14-inch rectangle. Brush with melted butter, leaving 1/2-inch border uncovered; sprinkle with brown sugar, pecan, cinnamon mixture. Starting at long side, tightly roll up, pinching seam to seal. Brush with melted butter. With serrated knife, cut into 16 pieces; place cut side down, in prepared pan. Cover and let rise for 1 hour or until doubled in volume. Meanwhile, preheat oven to 375F (190C).

Bake in preheated oven for 20 to 25 minutes, until golden brown. Let cool in pan for 3 minutes, then invert onto serving platter. Scrape remaining filling from the pan onto the buns. Makes 16 sticky buns.

mini butter pecan tarts

3 ounces (75 g) cream cheese
1/2 cup (125 mL) country fresh butter
1 cup (250 mL) all-purpose flour
1 1/2 cups (375 mL) brown sugar
2 tablespoons (30 mL) country fresh butter, melted
2 farm fresh eggs
pinch of Ontario salt
1 teaspoon (5 mL) pure vanilla extract
1/2 cup (125 mL) Northern pecans, chopped

Preheat oven to 350F (180C). In the bowl of an electric mixer, beat cream cheese and butter until creamy. Mix in flour and beat on low until mixture is smooth. Form into 24 balls. Spread 1 ball of dough around the inside of each mini tart cup. Set aside.

In the bowl of an electric mixer, beat brown sugar and butter. Add eggs one at a time, incorporating after each addition. Add salt and vanilla. Put a few chopped pecans in the bottom of each tart cup. Fill 3/4 full with filling and put a few more pecans on top. Bake for 30 minutes. Makes 24 mini tarts.

Ottawa

The Piggy Market
Open daily

David Neil first began as a market vendor at the Landsdowne Farmers' Market, selling his charcuterie. When he built up a loyal and large enough following, he open a store in downtown Ottawa. When I walked in I could smell the bacon that just came out of the smoker. Dave buys whole Tamworth heritage breed pigs from area farmers and uses almost every inch of the animal to make the most amazing products that range from bacon and paté to sausage and pepperoni. Dave shows his roots by showcasing local farmers on his 'Wall of Fame' inside the store. www.thepiggymarket.com

400 Winston Avenue, Ottawa

local food in

Muskoka

Muskoka is Ontario's quintessential cottage country, stretching from the northern tip of Lake Couchiching to Georgian Bay in the west and Algonquin Park in the east. Because more than two million visitors come to Muskoka each year, the culinary scene is surprisingly well developed with farmers, chefs and culinary entrepreneurs making a significant contribution to its delicious culture.

MUSKOKA FOOD

Artisan mushroom growers like Muskoka Shiitake, Muskoka Mushroom Farm and Edible Fungi characterize this region. These farms fill restaurant kitchens with their delicate, oak-log grown shiitake. Drive through the back roads during August and the chances are you'll be able to smell the garlic harvest. Big Ass Garlic and Muskoka Garlic are the two main growers you'll find at farmers' markets.

CULINARY ENTREPRENEURS

Huntsville has its fair share of culinary entrepreneurs: Bell Ice Cream Company that offers lusciously rich ice creams in locally inspired flavours; Springhill Freshwater Company bottles natural spring water that tastes clean, clear and refreshing; The Farmer's Daughter Market offers a variety of local foods and products handmade on-site under the Farmers' Daughter label; and the Bear Foot Gourmet in Baysville offers delicious local food prepared on premise for you to take away.

COOKING CLASSES

Brooklands Farm in Milford Bay offers cooking classes, gardening demos and an eclectic variety of vegetables, and Ivanita Farm and Meats has you covered with hormone-free, pastured beef, lamb, pork and poultry.

RESTAURANTS

One of the region's leading chefs, Rory Golden of the Deerhurst Resort, was one of the founding members of Savour Muskoka. He works with more than 20 area farmers to create his "eat local" menus. A few years ago Rory told me he was working with a farmer to develop a unique breed of cattle they were calling Muskoka Highland. It's still in the works, but it speaks to the culinary prowess of a region you probably only thought of as cottage country.

> Muskoka has a local food web directory, agriculture and culinary map, 10 farmers' markets and lots of markets on farms that offer fresh food in season.
>
> Savour Muskoka | www.savourmuskoka.com

pumpkin streusel muffin

1/2 cup (125 mL) sugar pumpkin purée
1/2 cup (125 mL) whole milk
1/3 cup (80 mL) Ontario vegetable oil
1/2 cup (125 mL) sugar
1 farm fresh egg, beaten
1 3/4 cups (430 mL) all-purpose flour
2 teaspoons (10 L) baking powder
1/2 teaspoon (2.5 mL) Ontario salt
1 teaspoon (5 mL) cinnamon
1/4 cup (60 mL) brown sugar
1/2 teaspoon (2.5 mL) cinnamon
2 tablespoons (30 mL) country fresh butter
1/3 cup (80 mL) orchard walnuts, chopped

Pre-heat oven to 400F (200C). In the bowl of an electric mixer, combine pumpkin, milk, oil, sugar and egg. Mix on medium until well blended. In another bowl, whisk together the flour, baking powder, salt and cinnamon. Add to mixture in blender and mix until batter is still a little lumpy.

Grease a 12-muffin tin. Pour batter into muffin cups to about 3/4 full. Combine brown sugar, cinnamon, butter and walnuts. Work the mixture until it resembles crumbs. Sprinkle streusel topping over muffins. Bake for 18 to 22 minutes, until golden brown. Serve warm. Makes 12 muffins.

Waterloo

NAUMAN'S FARM MARKET
Open seasonally from mid June to end of October

If you find a pumpkin farm, chances are you'll find a corn maze. For Hugh Nauman and his wife Ann, it's all about farm and country hospitality and Nauman's embraces so much more. It starts in mid June with luscious, juicy strawberries that go so well with their rhubarb. In the summer you'll find purple, black and yellow raspberries and in the fall, sweet corn and more than 20 varieties of pumpkins in every size and colour imaginable. In their on-farm market you will find it all along with freshly made pies. www.naumanfarm.com

3250 Hessen Strasse, St Clements

Eating local seems safer. We can see how a local farmer farms. That transparency doesn't exist with other foods.

Dessert: tree-ripened orchard fruit

featuring

enjoy with

MOON SHADOWS WINERY
Plum
www.moonshadowswinery.com

black plum tart

1 farm fresh egg
2 tablespoons (30 mL) milk
1/2 package puff pastry
2 tablespoons (30 mL) Ontario wine jelly
2 cups (500 mL) Ontario black plums,
pitted and sliced into quarters

In a small bowl, whisk together the egg and milk to make an egg wash. Set aside. On a lightly floured surface, roll out the puff pastry to form a 10-inch square. Cut 1/2-inch strips from each side of the puff pastry. Transfer pastry square to a baking sheet. Neatly brush a 1/2-inch wide border of egg wash along each edge of the puff pastry square. Top with corresponding pastry strips, pressing gently with your fingers to adhere. Using a fork, poke holes in the base of the dough. Transfer to refrigerator and chill for 1 hour.

Preheat oven to 400F (200C). Melt the wine jelly in the microwave for 1 minute on medium-high heat. Pour over the plums and toss to coat completely. Remove the pastry square from the refrigerator and pour the plums into the centre. Spread them around evenly over the pastry square. Brush edges of the pastry with egg glaze. Bake for 20 minutes or until the edges are puffed and golden brown. Makes one tart.

Niagara

HUGHES VINEYARD
Wholesale only

Once a popular caterer, Ed Hughes now tends his 24-acre vineyard. He has a good business selling juice to home winemakers and even offers interested customers their own row of vines to tend for their own wine. Then one day Ed's culinary and farming sensibilities came together and he began to make verjus. Verjus is tart grape juice made from unripe grapes. It's a great culinary ingredient that replaces lemon juice in most recipes, prevents oxidation of foods and is delicious in vinaigrettes and salad dressings. Louise Engle at Featherstone Winery even makes a refreshing summer drink from their verjus – it's delicious. Ed makes his verjus from pinot noir grapes. It has an intense fruity flavour with lots of pinot characteristics. You can buy it at many specialty food stores or through 100-km Foods. 100kmfoods.com | www.niagaracuisine.com

3874 Greenlane Road, Beamsville

enjoy with

KITTLING RIDGE WINERY
Icewine & Brandy
www.kittlingridge.com

apple sticky toffee pudding

1 cup (250 mL) Ontario apple cider
1/2 cup (125 mL) dried apples, chopped
2 teaspoons (10 mL) baking soda
3 tablespoons (45 mL) country fresh
butter, room temperature
1/2 cup (125 mL) sugar
2 farm fresh eggs
1 1/4 cups (310 mL) all-purpose flour
2 teaspoons (10 mL) baking powder
1 teaspoon (5 mL) ground cinnamon
1/2 teaspoon (2.5 mL) ground nutmeg
1 1/2 cups (375 mL) Spy apples, peeled and chopped
3/4 cup (180 mL) Northern pecans, chopped

Toffee Sauce
6 tablespoons (90 mL) country fresh butter
1/2 cup (125 mL) brown sugar
1/3 cup (80 mL) whipping cream
1 teaspoon (5 mL) pure vanilla extract

In a saucepan, bring cider and dried apples to a boil. Remove from heat, carefully stir in baking soda. Cool about 20 minutes.

Preheat oven to 350F (180C). Meanwhile, beat the butter and sugar until light. Add eggs, one at a time beating well. In a small bowl, whisk flour and spices. Add flour alternately to the butter mixture with cider and dried apples. Add chopped apples and pecans. Pour into a greased 9-inch pan or individual ramekins. Bake for 35 to 40 minutes or until set in the middle.

Melt butter in a saucepan. Add brown sugar and cook until sugar is dissolved. Add whipping cream slowly and simmer until slightly thickened. Remove from heat and stir in vanilla. Serve warm apple pudding drizzled with toffee sauce. Serves 6 to 8.

Lambton County

FOREST HILL ORCHARDS
Farmers' Market sales only

Melody & Rod Arnhold have spent their life farming. They have a 50-acre farm on a gravelly ridge overlooking Lake Huron. In this little micro climate they grow tender fruit; peaches, prune plums, nectarines, apricots and sweet cherries. They're trying their hand at quince this year. They also grow a small market garden to complement their farmers' market stands. You can find the Arnholds at the Grand Bend, Kitchener and Forest Farmers' Markets. On the farm they have a cider mill and each year they pride themselves on the freshest, sweetest apple cider in the county.

5577 Aberarder Line, Forest

apple terrine

3 tablespoons (45 mL) water
3/4 cup (180 mL) sugar
2 tablespoon (30 mL) Vidal ice syrup
2 tablespoons (30 mL) ground cinnamon
1/2 cup (125 mL) brown sugar, packed
8 apples (peeling is optional)
serve with Monforte Diary Gaperon cheese

Preheat oven to 300F (150C). Bring water and sugar to a simmer in a small saucepan over medium-high heat, stirring until sugar dissolves. Cook, swirling pan periodically until mixture turns dark amber. Remove from heat and add ice syrup. Pour into a 6 1/2-inch springform pan, swirling to coat bottom and sides.

Place cinnamon and brown sugar in a small bowl and mix well. Set aside. Start with 3 apples (to prevent them browning as you work). Using a mandoline or sharp knife, cut the apple into thin circular slices on one side, turn it around and make thin circular slices on the other side. Repeat with remaining apples.

Arrange 1 layer of apple slices in a tight, overlapping circle in the springform pan, covering the bottom completely. Sprinkle with 1 tablespoon of the cinnamon/sugar mixture and 1 teaspoon of ice syrup. Arrange next layer of apple slices in a tight, overlapping circle and sprinkle with 1 tablespoon of sugar mixture. Repeat slicing and layering with remaining apples and sugar/cinnamon mixture. Sprinkle ice syrup only on every second layer. Leave 1/2 inch of space at the top of pan.

Cover top and bottom (to catch the drips) of pan with foil. Place in a large roasting pan, and transfer to oven. Carefully pour boiling water into pan to come halfway up sides of springform pan. Bake for 1 1/2 hours or until apples are soft through. Transfer to a wire rack, uncover top foil and remove pan from bottom foil and reserve sauce. Let cool for 20 minutes.

Meanwhile, pour sauce into a small saucepan and boil until slightly thickened, about 5 minutes. Place a pie dish or a rimmed plate over the springform pan and quickly invert. Remove springform pan. Slice terrine and serve with warm sauce and a bit of cheese.

Prince Edward County

CAMPBELL'S ORCHARD
Open 7 days a week from 9 to 5:30

Second generation farmer Colin Campbell and his wife Diane grow apples in Carrying Place, in the northern part of what the locals refer to as 'the County'. In their on-farm market, you can buy apples all winter long, starting with just-picked Paula Red and Ginger Gold in September to the last of the last of the Empire, Delicious and Ida Red in May. In fact, apple and rhubarb are a delicious spring flavour combination. Throughout the summer you'll find all sorts of fruits and vegetables in their market along with apple cider, frozen summer fruit and more. www.campbellsorchards.com | www.harvestin.ca

1633 County Road E, Carrying Place

enjoy with
FIVE ROWS CRAFT WINE
Pinot Gris
www.fiverows.com

cherry custard tart

1 recipe essential custard, page 296
1 essential pastry tart shell, page 297
1/2 cup (125 mL) Ontario black cherry jam
16 firm, sweet Ontario cherries with stems

Melt the black cherry jam in a microwave for 1 minute. Stir well and brush over the bottom of the cooled tart shell. Pour the cooled custard into the tart shell. Press a layer of plastic wrap over the top of the custard so it doesn't form a film. Refrigerate for an hour. When ready to serve, line up the cherries on top of the tart. Serves 8.

Ontario

FARMERS' MARKETS ONTARIO®

Before there were supermarkets, people would congregate at a central meeting place to buy from local farmers bearing bushels of just-picked produce, as well as butchers and bakers offering their freshest wares. These marketplaces were the hearts and hubs of their communities: where neighbours would meet and mingle, socializing with each other and with the people producing their food. Today, farmers' markets perform the same role, bringing town and country together and ensuring easy access to nutritious locally grown food. But not all vendors are farmers, so look for the MyPick® Verified Local Farmer® symbol. It identifies real farmers who sell only what they grow. Today, farmers' markets are popping up all across Ontario, and they're still about connecting— to the land, to each other, and to a better quality of life. To find a market near you, visit the website.

www.farmersmarketsontario.com

enjoy with

VILLA NOVA ESTATE WINERY
Cerise
www.villanovaestatewinery.com

cherry mousse

1 cup (250 mL) fresh sweet cherries, pitted
2 tablespoons (30 mL) Ontario dry white wine
1/2 cup (125 mL) sugar
1 teaspoon (5 mL) Niagara verjus
1 envelope unflavoured gelatin
1 teaspoon (5 mL) country fresh butter,
room temperature
1 cup (250 mL) whipping cream
1 teaspoon (5 mL) pure vanilla extract
1 farm fresh egg white
2 teaspoons (10 mL) sugar
3-1/2 tablespoons (53 mL) all-purpose flour
1 teaspoon (5 mL) pure vanilla extract
4 tablespoons (60 mL) country fresh butter, softened

In a saucepan combine pitted cherries, wine and sugar. Cook over medium heat until cherries are soft and sugar has dissolved. Add verjus and sprinkle gelatin over top. Bring to a slow boil, stirring constantly. Pour into a bowl and refrigerate until it becomes thick and syrupy but not quite set.

Meanwhile, butter 6 ramekins and set aside. Whip cream with vanilla to soft peak stage. Gently fold cream into the chilled cherry gelatin mixture. Spoon into ramekins and refrigerate until set.

Meanwhile, make the touile. In a small mixing bowl whip the egg white with sugar until stiff and glossy. Add the flour, vanilla and butter, mixing at low speed until well blended. Line a baking sheet with parchment paper and draw 6 circles on the parchment. Using a spoon, spread the dough evenly over the circles.

Bake in a preheated 350F (180C) oven for 7 to 10 minutes or until lightly browned around the edges. Remove from oven and let cool slightly before transferring to a cooling rack. To serve, unmould each cherry mousse onto a dessert dish and top with cookie. Serves 6.

Kawartha Lakes

KAWARTHA DAIRY
Open daily year round

Summer cottagers were the first to discover Kawartha Dairy. It become a long standing tradition to pick up this delicious ice cream on their way to the cottage and always on their way home. This artisan dairy run by Jack and Ila Crowe was a small dairy when they purchased it in 1937. Back then the dairy got its milk from surrounding dairy farms and it's pretty much the same today, with Jack making sure they get their supply of fresh, creamy milk on a daily basis. Today, Kawartha Dairy has retail stores in Bobcaygeon, Minden, Bancroft, Kawartha Lakes, Uxbridge, Huntsville and Peterborough. I'm thinking they don't want to miss any cottagers. It's also available at an independent grocer near you. Check out the website. www.kawarthadairy.com

89 Prince Street, Bobcaygeon

Ottawa

ALPENBLICK FARM
Open year round, call first, 613-253-2640.

Robert Oechsli and Petra Stevenson own a 250-acre organic farm. Open the gate at the street and drive in but make sure you close the gate behind you because the animals roam freely on the property. There are over 100 animals including beef cattle, a few dairy cows, sheep and goats for cheese making. The day I was there, chef and restaurant owner Roger Weldon of Ballygibbins in Carleton Place was doing some negotiating over some farm fresh produce. Robert makes a very small amount of goats cheese that is in high demand, so good luck trying to get some. And he has no plans to increase the quantity because he believes it will decrease the quality. Robert's message to everyone is to "know where your food comes from." www.savourottawa.ca

8138 Golf Club Way, Ashton

peach & riesling gelatin

1 1/2 envelopes unflavoured gelatin
1 cup (250 mL) cold water
2 cups (500 mL) late harvest riesling wine
1/4 cup (60 mL) sugar
2 tree-ripened peaches, pitted and sliced
3/4 cup (180 mL) + 1 1/2 tablespoons (22.5 mL) sugar
2 tree-ripened peaches, pitted and sliced
sprigs of mint for garnish

In a large bowl, sprinkle the gelatin over cold water and let stand for 5 minutes to soften. Meanwhile, in a saucepan, bring the wine, sugar and peaches to a boil. Reduce the heat and simmer for 10 minutes. Pour the hot wine mixture through a strainer into the gelatin and mash the peaches to release all their juices. Stir the mixture until the gelatin is dissolved.

Divide the gelatin among 4 ramekins and chill until set, about 5 hours. When ready to serve, sprinkle the sugar over the peach slices and toss to coat. Dip the bottom of each mold into a bowl of warm water for 5 seconds and invert onto chilled dessert plates. Spoon the peaches around each Riesling gelatin and serve. Serves 8.

peach and strawberry semifreddo

1 cup (250 mL) strawberries, puréed
3 ripe peaches, peeled, pitted and puréed
2 tablespoons (30 mL) corn starch
1/2 cup (125 mL) apple juice
1/2 cup (125 mL) sugar
1/3 cup (80 mL) Roman Cheese fresh ricotta cheese
1/3 cup (80 mL) Woolwich Dairy soft white goat's cheese
1 cup (250 mL) whipping cream
3 tablespoons (45 mL) icing sugar

Put the strawberry purée in a saucepan. Put the peach puréed in a separate saucepan. Dissolve the corn starch in the apple juice and pour half of it into the strawberries and the other half in the peaches. Divide the sugar between both saucepans and warm gently, stirring each until thickened.

Remove from heat and to the warm peaches, add the ricotta cheese. Stir until well blended and set aside until it reaches room temperature. To the strawberries, add the goat's cheese. Stir until well blended and set aside until it reaches room temperature.

Whip the cream with sugar until soft peaks form. Add half the whipped cream to the cooled strawberry mixture and carefully fold in. Add the other half to the peach mixture and carefully fold in.

Spoon the strawberry mixture into 8 individual glass dessert cups filling only half way up the cup. Fill dessert cups with peach mixture. Chill until ready to serve. Garnish with whole strawberries and peach slices. Serves 8.

Huron County

100-MILE PRODUCE
Mid May to Christmas

You'll find Robert Foreman at the Keady and St Jacobs Farmers' Market all summer and fall with tables full of a wide variety of garden vegetables. What Robert doesn't grow on his 38.5-acre farm, he gathers from 8 Amish families all in the Belgrave area or buys from the Elmira Produce Auction. Robert grew up on a farm and this 5th generation farm returned to the land because, as he puts it, "it's in my blood." You can buy directly from the farm when you see Robert's front yard piled with sweet corn, pumpkins and squash. Just put your money in the honour box on the stand.

85476 London Rd (Hwy 4), Belgrave

enjoy with

PINE FARMS WINERY
Hard Apple Cider
www.pinefarmsorchard.com

local food in

Oxford County

I love driving through country roads filled with people making a living off the land. It's not unusual to find yourself behind a wagon filled with hay, large trucks busy with farm work kicking up clouds of dust and animals wandering the meadows and hills. Make sure you bring a camera because you never know when farm and country life will inspire a few beautiful photos.

LOCAL PRODUCTS

In almost every region in Ontario you'll find sweet things happening. From apiaries and home honey producers to sugar bushes and maple syrup makers, you need to try them all. These home grown farm products are all based on the creative approach of the producers and they differ vastly between regions and between farmers in the same region. This makes them as exciting and diverse as Ontario's wines and cheeses.

Woodstock is a busy city and in the heart of one of their busiest commerce streets sits a monument to Springbank Snow Countess. She's a dairy cow and in her time, was the county's largest butterfat producer (weighing in at 9,062 pounds of butterfat and 207,505 pounds of milk during her lifetime). Oxford is Ontario's dairy capital and it was once home to at least 92 cheese factories.

Oxford also used to be tobacco territory, but vast fields of potatoes and trout farms now replace tobacco fields. Drive the rural roads and chances are you'll find small black covered wagons pulled by horses, because this is Mennonite country. You'll find hard-core cooperative agriculture practiced here, creating a strong farm and country ambience that visitors love. It's a reminder of how pure and good fresh food from the farm can be.

RESTAURANTS

Chefs like Eric Boyar can easily get caught up in the region's agricultural offerings. In the converted house on Peel Street, in the heart of Woodstock, he runs Six Thirty Nine Restaurant. He uses a base of local food to form his menus. When Jon and I dined, we sat at the chef's table, a beautiful wooden bar that overlooks all the action in the kitchen and offers a front row seat for the wafting smells – yum! Behind the kitchen, we saw Eric's bike with bags of produce; he had just returned from the market and everything was fresh, including the trout from nearby Goossens Trout Farm. It's not unusual to find curious farmers dining here just to see what Eric is creating with their produce.

DINNER THEATRE

In the little town of Bright is a quaint farm dinner theatre. The Walters family has converted a large barn into a comfortable theatre producing world-class performances of music and comedy. Parking on the stunningly beautiful grounds seems wrong, but this is country life, so just watch out for the trees. A local caterer, Quehl's of Tavistock, prepares the dinners with a flair for local flavours.

FARM SHOW

Canada's Outdoor Farm Show is in Oxford County and takes place on the fairgrounds on Highway 59. It's Canada's largest outdoor farm show. Plan on attending, and if you need a room for the night, call Bon Air Bed and Breakfast, a restored farm now running as a bed and breakfast. A little known fact is that Gerald and Danielle Kennedy have transformed the top of their silo into an amazing observatory; ask them for some sky-time and experience farm country hospitality with a 'sky's the limit' promise.

Oxford County has a local food web directory, agriculture and culinary map, farmers' markets and lots of markets on farms that offer fresh food in season.

Oxfordlicious | www.oxfordlicious.com
Buy Local Oxford | www.oxfordbuylocal.ca
Oxford Fresh | www.oxfordfresh.com

peach ice cream cake

6 tree-ripened peaches, peeled and pitted
1 tablespoon (15 mL) sugar
24 ladyfingers
1 recipe essential custard, cooled, page 296
1 recipe essential caramel ice cream, softened, page 296
2 tree-ripened peaches, pitted and sliced thinly for garnish

Trim the bottom of each ladyfinger and line the sides of a 9-inch springform pan by standing them, cut-side down vertically, edge to edge, along the inside rim of the pan. Set aside.

In a blender, purée peaches with sugar. Set aside. To the custard add half the peach purée. Mix to combine and chill. Pour the peach custard into an ice cream maker and make according to manufacturer's instructions. When ice cream is done, spread evenly in springform pan, smoothing the top. Place a sheet of plastic wrap directly on the surface of the peach ice cream and freeze for 2 hours.

Remove from freezer and pour remaining peach purée over top. Smooth and return to freezer. Freeze until firm, about 2 hours.

Soften caramel cream ice cream and spread a generous half on top of the peach purée. Smooth the top and return to the freezer until frozen, about 6 to 8 hours. Remove and quickly arrange peach slices in a circular motion around the edge of the cake. Return to freezer.

When ready to serve, remove cake from freezer and let stand at room temperature 5 to 10 minutes. Remove pan rim. To slice cake neatly, dip the blade of a large knife in hot water and wipe it dry before cutting each slice. Serve immediately.

Essex County

MELEG'S LAKEVIEW ORCHARD
Open daily, 9 to 6

Tom and John Meleg are the owners of a 65-acre farm that produces peaches in Essex County, Ontario's warmest growing region. They're sweet, juicy and exciting eaten out of hand and also made into many scrumptious desserts. Their largest orchard happens to be apples. They grow lots of different varieties of apples and apple products like farm-made apple pies, both fresh and frozen from their on-site bakery, candy apples, apple pie filling in jars that fill one pie and apple butter to spread on your morning toast for that fresh country flavour. In the on-site farmers' market you can also find other produce grown on the farm from orchard fruit, watermelon and honeydew to lots of vegetables.

158 Arner Townline, Kingsville

enjoy with

COX CREEK CELLARS
Russet Fantasy
www.coxcreekcellars.on.ca

rhubarb applesauce tart

5 fresh rhubarb stalks, 9-inches long
1/4 cup (60 mL) sugar
3 Royal Gala apples, or your favourite cooking apple
1/4 cup (60 mL) brown sugar
2 tablespoons (30 mL) country butter, melted
2 cups (500 mL) home made applesauce
1 recipe essential tart shell, cooled, page 297
pinch of cinnamon
1/2 cup (125 mL) sugar

Heat the oven to 400F (200C). Toss rhubarb in sugar and roast for 15 minutes. Meanwhile, peel, core and very thinly slice the apples. Toss with the brown sugar and the melted butter. Spread the applesauce in the base of the cooled, baked tart shell, push rhubarb pieces into the applesauce and arrange the sliced apples over top. Brush the apple with any butter and sugar remaining in the bottom of the bowl and lightly dust with cinnamon.

Bake until the apple slices are very soft and golden, about 25 minutes. Remove from the oven and cool slightly. Serve warm or completely cool for a firmer tart. Makes 1 tart.

Essex County

MARIA SIMONE
Farm stand open daily in season

Maria Simone runs a small vegetable farm by Leamington standards but big enough for Maria who has tended the 34-acre farm since her husband passed away over 34 years ago. This proud Portuguese woman along with three Mexican helpers manage apple, pear and peach orchards and fields of green and yellow beans, peppers, eggplant, beets, cucumbers, cherry peppers, garlic, tomatillos, tomatoes, onions, potatoes, squash, sweet corn, melons cabbage and cauliflower. She sells a lot from her sexy farm stand and the rest she ships off to Montreal for eager foodies who appreciate good food.

2644 County Road #20, Harrow

sugared apricot tart

8 orchard apricots, pitted, peeled and halved
3 tablespoons (45 mL) Niagara verjus
1 recipe essential custard, cooled, page 296
1 recipe essential tart shell, cooled, page 297
1/2 cup (125 mL) just-picked Ontario blueberries
2 tablespoons (30 mL) coarse sugar

Place the apricots in a bowl and drizzle with verjus. Set aside and occasionally baste with verjus from the bottom of the bowl.

To assemble the tart, pour the cool custard into the tart shell. Press a layer of plastic wrap over the top of the custard so it doesn't form a film. Refrigerate for an hour. Remove from the refrigerator, remove plastic wrap and press the apricots, cut side down onto the custard, top with blueberries and sprinkle with coarse sugar. Refrigerate until ready to serve. Makes 1 tart.

enjoy with

MONRO'S MEADERY
Sweet Mead
www.monrohoney.com

Essex County

SIMPSON'S ORCHARD
Open year round on the farm 9 to 5, closed Sundays

Wally and Debbie Simpson are carrying on a farming tradition with their family. The farm, established in 1921, boasts an orchard with apples, peaches, pears and cherries as well as quince, blueberries and amazing apricots. The orchard harvest takes place from mid July to August and the blueberry harvest is in July and August. As for field crops, the Simpsons grow sweet melons and watermelons along with potatoes, squash, sweet potatoes, sweet corn and more. You'll also find dried apples, apple butter, apple sauce and caramel apples in their on-farm market.

239 County Road 5, Leamington

Chatham-Kent County

DELHAVEN ORCHARDS
On-farm market open year round, 7 days a week from July to October, closed Sunday in winter

Hector Delanghe is a second generation farmer who started farming when he was 15 years old. Now in his early '70s, Hector is still farming while his son Mark is gradually taking over more of the tender fruit business. "When you look at my farm and the market, you're looking at my life," says Hector. From apples to peaches, nectarines to sweet and sour cherries, you can buy from the on-farm market along with sweet potatoes, tomatoes and onions from neighbouring farms. In the winter you can buy pails of frozen pitted cherries, apple cider and fresh apples. www.delhaven.com

8182 Talbot Trail, Blenheim

sweet cherry clafoutis

1 pound (.45 kg) sweet Ontario cherries, pitted
1/4 cup (60 mL) sugar
1/2 cup (125 mL) all-purpose flour, plus more for dusting
Pinch of Ontario salt
3 farm fresh eggs, lightly beaten
2 cups (500 mL) whole milk
3 tablespoons (45 mL) country fresh butter, softened,
plus more to smear on the dish
1 teaspoon (5 mL) pure vanilla extract
1 tablespoon (15 mL) sugar
1 tablespoon (15 mL) country fresh butter
Icing sugar for dusting

In a bowl, toss the cherries with 3 tablespoons of sugar. Set aside.

In another bowl, whisk the flour and salt. Whisk in the eggs and set aside. In a small saucepan, heat the milk with the butter until the butter melts. Whisk a bit of the warm milk into the flour mixture just until smooth. Whisk in the remaining milk. Add the vanilla, cover and let rest at room temperature for at least 1 hour.

Preheat the oven to 425F (220C). Butter a 9 1/2-inch deep-dish pie plate or individual ramekins and dust with flour. Spread the cherries in a single layer in the pie plate, adding any sugar from the baking sheet to the cherries. Whisk the batter again and pour it over the cherries.

Bake the clafoutis just above the cente of the oven for 20 minutes, or until the top is just set and golden. Top with the sugar and butter. Bake for 10 to 15 minutes longer, or until a knife inserted in the centre comes out clean. Transfer to a rack to cool. Dust with icing sugar, cut into wedges. Serves 4 to 6.

enjoy with

RUSH CREEK WINERY
Cassis
www.rushcreekwines.ca

enjoy with

COLANERI ESTATE WINERY
Profundo
www.colaneriwines.com

yellow plum souffle

2/3 cup (160 mL) sugar
2 tablespoons (30 mL) country fresh butter, room temperature
3 farm fresh eggs, separated
3 tablespoons (45 mL) all-purpose flour
1/2 cup (125 mL) yellow plum purée
1 cup (250 mL) whole milk
dash Ontario salt
1/8 teaspoon (.7 mL) cream of tartar

Preheat oven to 350F (160C). In a mixing bowl, beat together the sugar and butter until creamy. Beat in the egg yolks one at a time. Gradually stir in flour, alternating with the yellow plum purée and milk; stir until well blended. In a medium mixing bowl, beat egg whites until foamy. Add salt and cream of tartar. Continue beating until the form soft peaks.

Fold egg whites gently into the plum mixture, just until incorporated throughout the batter. Pour into a 1 1/2-quart souffle dish. Set souffle dish in a larger pan with about 1-inch of hot water. Bake until top is set, about 35 to 45 minutes. Serve pudding hot with sauce. Serves 4 to 6.

Yellow Plum Purée: Pit and quarter 6 yellow plums. Put them in a heavy bottom saucepan with ¼ cup (60 mL) sugar and 2 tablespoons (30 mL) Ontario honey. Bring to a boil, reduce heat and simmer for 5 minutes or until plums are soft. Set aside to cool. Purée in a blender. Makes 1 cup of purée.

Niagara

KURTZ ORCHARDS
Open daily, 9 – 7 in season

The Kurtz farm is on the picture perfect Niagara River Parkway in Niagara-on-the-Lake. From the 50-acre working farm they grow orchard fruit like peaches, cherries, apricots, nectarines and lots of yellow plums. The Kurtz family uses most of their fruit to create delicious jams, preserves and other gourmet foods that you'll find in the large retail barn. Stop by for a visit, enjoy lunch from the farm kitchen and walk the beautiful grounds. In the evenings take in a complimentary cooking class or collect their recipe cards found throughout the store. Meet all 3 generation of Kurtz as they work hard to bring you farm grown gourmet foods. www.kurtzorchards.com, www.niagaraculinarytrail.com

16006 Niagara River Parkway, Niagara-on-the-Lake

Farmers get a much better price selling their produce directly. Not only do they obtain about double the price at the farmers' market than they would if they sold to the supermarket, but they enjoy the contact with the townsfolk who are so eager for their produce.

Dessert: on the sweeter side

featuring

blueberry cheesecake

2-1/2 cups (625 mL) Ontario ricotta cheese
8 oz (225 g) cream cheese
1 cup (250 mL) sugar
1 tablespoon (15 mL) cornstarch
4 farm fresh eggs
1 teaspoon (5 mL) pure vanilla extract
1/2 cup (125 mL) Ontario sour cream
2 cups (500 mL) fresh picked blueberries

Preheat oven to 350F (180C). Place ricotta and cream cheese in a food processor and process until smooth, Add sugar and cornstarch. Process until well combined. Add eggs one at a time and process until smooth. Add vanilla and sour cream and process until soft and silky. Pour half of the batter into a 9-inch springform pan and spread two thirds of the blueberries on top of the batter. Pour the remaining batter on top of the blueberries, shake the pan gently to level and decorate the top with remaining blueberries. Bake for 1 hour and 15 minutes or until set. Remove from oven and place on a wire rack to completely cool. Makes 1 cheesecake.

Niagara

BLUEMIN' ACRES
Open during blueberry season

Diana and Edward DiMarco bought a 5-acre blueberry field in 1997 and have been producing heavy crops of deep, black, large blueberries each season. On average, Bluemin' Acres produces approximately 10 tons of the black pearls in a season. You can purchase blueberries by weight, from the barn on the property so feel free to bring your own containers or use the containers Diana supplies. Besides blueberries, you can also buy blackberries, Saskatoon berries, red currents, green and red gooseberries, rhubarb and apples in season.

1007 Line #1, Niagara-on-the-Lake

raspberry meringue pudding

4 small brioche or egg rolls, broken into pieces
2 cups (500 mL) whole country milk
3 tablespoons (45 mL) Niagara verjus, ice syrup or maple syrup
2 tablespoons (30 mL) country fresh butter
4 farm fresh eggs, separated
1/2 cup (125 mL) sugar
1/2 cup (125 mL) Ontario raspberry jam
2 cups (500 mL) just-picked raspberries
1/2 cup (125 mL) sugar
pinch of cream of tartar
2 tablespoons (30 mL) sugar

Preheat oven to 350F (180C). Butter 4 large individual ramekins and pack the brioche into the ramekins so they are half full. In a small saucepan over medium high heat, bring milk, verjus and butter almost to a boil. It's ready when tiny bubbles form along the sides of the saucepan. Turn off the heat. Meanwhile, beat egg yolks with sugar until thick and golden. Drizzle the hot milk mixture slowly over the egg yolks, beating constantly. Pour the custard over the brioche and let sit to soak for 5 minutes. Place the ramekins on a baking sheet and bake for 20 to 25 minutes or until the brioche is golden and puffed up (it will collapse when cooled).

Meanwhile bubble raspberry jam with the fresh raspberries for 2 minutes in a shallow pan over low heat. Remove from heat. When the brioche has a few minutes left in the oven, whisk the egg whites in a bowl with the cream of tartar and sugar until they form peaks. Spoon the warm raspberries onto the brioche pudding and top with frothy egg whites. Scatter each with a little sugar, then bake for 15 minutes or until golden. Serves 4.

Ottawa Valley

ACORN CREEK GARDEN FARM
Open 7 days a week, year round from 8 to 6

Andy and Cindy Terauds work their 100-acre farm in Carp. You can find Andy at the Ottawa Farmers' Market at Landsdowne Park, at the Carp Farmers' Market or you can visit the retail market on the farm (call for winter hours, 613-836-2613). Andy grows over 850 varieties of vegetables including beautiful multi-coloured carrots, 129 different varieties of melons and 160 different types of peppers including some of the hottest in the world. On Labour Day Monday the Terauds open their farm and offer a MelonFest & Pepper Pow Wow complete with farm tours, field tastings and cooking demos by some of the restaurants that buy Acorn Creek produce. Don't miss it! www.acorncreek.com

928 Oak Creek Road, Carp

strawberry fool

2 cups (500 mL) just-picked field strawberries
1/2 cup (125 mL) icing sugar
2 tablespoons (30 mL) Niagara verjus
1/4 cup (60 mL) fruit sugar
1 cup (250 mL) whipping cream
1 cup (250 mL) extra thick yogurt

In a food processor, purée three quarters of the strawberries with the icing sugar and verjus until smooth. Finely dice the remaining strawberries and sprinkle with fruit sugar. In a large bowl, whip the cream until it forms soft peaks, add the yogurt, then beat until it thickens. Fold in the strawberry purée and diced strawberries. Do not fold to completely mix.

Pour into 4 or 6 wineglasses or dessert bowls. Refrigerate until set, about an hour. Serves 4 to 6.

enjoy with
SCOTCH BLOCK WINERY
Strawberry Sunsation
www.scotchblockwinery.com

Nipissing County

LEISURE FARMS
Open weekends for fall activities from 11 to 5

It's a large berry farm that stretches along the lovely banks of the Sturgeon River and during berry season dozens upon dozens of people can be seen loitering in the berry patches, picking their own sweet juicy berries. Second generation farmers Michael and Diane DesChatelets run the 250-acre farm with their son Mitch in Nipissing County. There is an on-farm market with a bakery that offers fresh-baked fruit pies and pastries. This is where you'll also find their award winning jam. In the fall you can get your fill of fresh corn and pumpkins with more family activities like wagon rides, marshmallow roasts, a haunted barn and a few corn and straw mazes. www.leisurefarms.ca

744 Quesnel Road, Sturgeon Falls

local food in

Grey & Bruce County

This region is home to the Bruce Trail and the Bruce Peninsula and is one of natural beauty. Tobermory at the top of the Bruce Peninsula is where the Niagara Escarpment ends and all along it are breathtaking vistas of land and water.

APPLE COUNTRY

It's also the region where the majority of Ontario's apples are grown. Along with the warmth from both Lake Huron and the Georgian Bay, it moderates temperatures and inspires a wealth of agriculture.

There is a whopping 7,500 acres of apple orchards in Thornbury, through the Beaver Valley and into smaller areas around Collingwood and Meaford. Traditionally known for McIntosh and heritage varieties like Northern Spy, the region's orchards have added newer, sweeter varieties like Honeycrisp, Ambrosia and Gala. In these areas, some 160 growers produce 25% of the province's total apple crop, with Meaford holding the title of Apple Capitol of Ontario.

APPLE PIE TRAIL

This is the home of the Blue Mountain Apple Pie Trail, a circuit of restaurants, orchards and markets showcasing everything apple – from pies and dumplings to cider and crepes.

CITRUS OF THE NORTH

It's in this region where the Sea Buckthorn berry grows. This tiny yellow berry is highly nutritious and very acidic, prompting locals to call it the 'citrus of the north'. The tartness of the fruit goes well when paired with other flavours – from tangy apple tarts to luxurious cheesecake.

With hundreds of small meat producers in the region, you'll find lots of small abattoirs and butcher shops housed in towns and villages throughout the region. A wide variety of meats are available, including pastured beef and specialty meats like elk, bison, emu, pheasant and award winning Wagyu beef.

Two First Nation fisheries provide fresh and smoked whitefish. Look for signs announcing local fish fries around Wiarton, which, by the way, is also home to the weather predicting groundhog, Wiarton Willie.

WINE

There are three wineries in this region, Georgian Hills Vineyards (www.georgianhillsvineyards.ca), Coffin Ridge Vineyard & Winery (www.coffinridge.ca) and Carrick Wines & Ciders (www.carrickwines.ca).

The Beaver River runs through the downtown area, filled with historic buildings, artisan shops and quaint food markets. Where the Saugeen and Teeswater Rivers meet is another country town worth exploring. Paisley is just southeast of Port Elgin and is a very pretty little town known as Bruce County's Heritage Village. Packed with gracious century homes, Paisley's historic downtown area is brimming with farm and country conviviality.

As with other regions, celebrations abound, everything from church suppers to agricultural fairs, maple syrup festivals, Pumpkinfest in Port Elgin, Field to Fork Feasts and of course the Taste of Blue and Apple Harvest Festival at The Village at Blue Mountain. (http://applepietrail.ca/events)

Grey Bruce has a local food web directory, a local agriculture and culinary map, an Apple Pie Trail, 15 farmers' markets and lots of on farm markets that offer fresh food in season.

Food Link Grey Bruce
| www.foodlinkgreybruce.com

Apple Pie Trail | www.applepietrail.ca

blueberry crumb squares

1 cup (250 mL) sugar
2-1/2 cups (625 mL) all-purpose flour
1 pinch ground cinnamon
1-1/4 cups (310 mL) country fresh butter, cold
1 farm fresh egg, beaten
1 teaspoon (5 mL) baking powder
pinch of salt
4 cups (1L) just-picked blueberries
1 tablespoon (15 mL) Ontario sweet white wine
1/2 cup (125 mL) sugar
3 teaspoons (15 mL) cornstarch

Preheat the oven to 375F (190C). Grease a 9 x 13"-inch pan. In a medium bowl, stir together sugar, flour and cinnamon. Using a fork or pastry cutter, cut in the butter and then the beaten egg. Divide mixture in half and to the generous half, add baking powder and salt (dough will be crumbly) and pat it into the prepared pan.

In another bowl, mix the blueberries with sweet wine to completely coat them. Stir together the sugar and cornstarch and sprinkle over the wet blueberries. Stir gently to completely coat the berries in the sugar mixture. Spoon the blueberry mixture evenly over the crust. Crumble remaining dough over the berry layer.

Bake in preheated oven for 50 minutes or until top is slightly brown. Cool completely before cutting into squares. Makes 16 squares.

Oxford County

KENT KREEK BERRIES
Open in season

Jeff and Paula Zelem started off with a small blueberry patch in 1984 and today they have 6 acres of blueberries, 2 acres of strawberries, 2 acres of raspberries and 2 acres of pumpkins, gourds and squash. The blueberries are large and lush, the strawberries juicy and aromatic, the corn sweet and crisp and the raspberries tender and ambrosial. The Zelem family has a passion for growing for flavour and culinary enjoyment. You can buy all of this plus pumpkins, gourds and squash from the little fruit stand at the entrance of the Kent Kreek Berry Farm run by Jeff, Paula and their four children. www.kentkreekberries.com

3173 Highway 3 West, Simcoe

Halton Hills

ANDREWS SCENIC ACRES
Open daily from May to October from 8 to 6

Laurie and Bert Andrews grow berries on their 100-acre farm, lots and lots of berries; 35 acres of strawberries, 21 acres of red and black raspberries, 14 acres of blueberries, gooseberries, elderberries, red and black currants, hayberries and Saskatoon berries. The Andrews are the berry experts of their region offering just-picked when in season and frozen year round. You can buy fresh baked pies, tarts and jam in their on-farm market or wonderful fruit wines in the winery, Scotch Block Winery. You can find them at the Milton, Georgetown, Brampton, Nathan Phillips Square and Sherway Gardens Farmers' Markets. www.andrewsscenicacres.com

9365 10th Sideroad, Milton

raspberry profiteroles

1/2 cup (125 mL) all-purpose flour
1 teaspoon (5 mL) sugar
pinch of Ontario salt
1/4 cup (60 mL) country fresh butter
1/2 cup (125 mL) water
2 farm fresh eggs
1 farm fresh egg, beaten
pinch of Ontario salt
1 cup (250 mL) Ontario field raspberries
1/4 cup (60 mL) sugar
2 teaspoons (10 mL) Niagara verjus
Ontario fresh raspberry ice cream

Preheat oven to 400F (200C). Put the flour, sugar and salt in a bowl and whisk to combine. In a heavy saucepan, bring the butter and water to a boil. Remove from heat and quickly stir in the flour mixture with a wooden spoon. Return to the heat and stir constantly until the dough begins to come away from the sides of the pan and forms a thick smooth ball, approximately 2 minutes. Let cool to lukewarm. Transfer to an electric mixer and beat in eggs until you have a thick glossy paste. Spoon 12 mounds of dough onto a parchment lined baking sheet, an inch apart. Whisk the egg and salt together and brush gently on tops of the dough. Bake for 15 minutes, reduce oven temperature to 350F (180C) and bake for an additional 30 to 40 minutes or until they're golden. Turn the oven off, open the door slightly and let the shells dry out for 15 minutes. Remove from oven and cool on a wire rack. Makes 12 profiteroles.

Put the raspberries, sugar and verjus in a heavy saucepan and bring to a boil. Stir to dissolve sugar and immediately remove from heat. Allow to cool and mash slightly. Makes about 1 cup.

Just before serving, slice profiteroles in half. Place a scoop of ice cream on the bottom of each profiterole and replace the top. Drizzle with raspberry sauce and serve immediately.

triple berry ice cream

1 cup (250 mL) whole milk
1 cup (250 mL) whipping cream
3 farm fresh egg yolks
1/2 cup (125 mL) sugar
1 cup (250 mL) fresh field strawberries, hulled and halved
1 cup (250 mL) fresh picked blueberries
1 cup (250 mL) fresh picked raspberries
1/4 cup (60 mL) sugar

In a heavy saucepan, place the milk and half of the cream. Cook over medium heat until bubbles form around the edges of the pan. Meanwhile, whisk the egg yolks, sugar and remaining cream in a bowl until sugar dissolves. Remove the milk from the heat and gradually drizzle a bit of the hot milk into the egg mixture, whisking continuously. Add more hot milk a bit at a time until half the hot milk is used. Gradually pour the egg mixture into the saucepan with the remaining hot milk while whisking. Cook over medium low heat, stirring constantly with a wooden spoon until thick enough to coat the back of the spoon, about 6 minutes. Remove from heat.

Meanwhile, put the berries and sugar in a food processor and process until smooth. Add the berry purée to the custard and stir to combine. Cover with plastic wrap to prevent a skin from forming and refrigerate until completely cooled, about an hour.

Pour the berry custard into an ice cream machine and make according to manufacturer's instructions. Makes about 1 quart.

Simcoe County

THUNDER BEACH BERRY FARM
Open daily during berry season

The land has been in Marcel Genier's family for 3 generations. He and wife, Corinne now have the responsibility of looking after his family legacy and his ancestors would be proud. Marcel and Corinne grow strawberries, raspberries and blueberries and have just planted an orchard of apples, pears and plums. What Marcel and Corinne love most are the returning customers who come back year after year to pick their own berries, bring their family and visitors and enjoy the Geniers' genuine farm and country conviviality. You will love the experience too!
www.tbbf.ca | www.ontariofarmfresh.com

1369 County Road 6, Lafontaine

Essex County

WINDSOR SALT
Available at most grocery stores

Windsor Salt is an internationally successful company in Essex County producing over 200 different kinds of salt. Salt is clearly one of the most widely-used minerals in the world. It's indispensible in the kitchen enhancing the flavour of so many foods. I love coarse salt for brining. Brine a chicken and you end up with a moister chicken when it is cooked. It does this by changing the structure of the muscle tissue in the meat which allows it to swell and absorb water and flavourings. No more dried out turkey or chicken once you master the art of brining all of your meats. It's also a great flavour contrast with sweet flavours like this caramel cheesecake.
www.windsorsalt.com

200 Morton Drive, Windsor

salted caramel cheesecake

8 ounces (225 g) cream cheese, room temperature
1/2 cup (125 mL) sugar
3 farm fresh eggs
1/2 cup (125 mL) sour cream
6 tablespoons (90 mL) corn syrup
1/2 cup (125 mL) sugar
3 tablespoons (45 mL) country fresh butter
1/2 cup (125 mL) whipping cream
1 teaspoon (5 mL) Ontario salt
coarse salt for garnish
mint sprigs

Preheat the oven to 325F (120C). In a large bowl, beat the cream cheese and sugar at medium speed until smooth. Beat in the eggs, 1 at a time. Beat in the sour cream. Pour the batter into six ramekins or custard cups.

Set the ramekins in a small pan and set the pan in the centre of the oven. Add enough hot water to the pan to reach halfway up the sides of the ramekins. Bake the cheesecakes for 15 minutes, or until set. Turn off the oven and leave the cheesecakes in for 1 hour. Transfer the ramekins to a rack and let cool completely. Store in the refrigerator until ready to use.

Meanwhile, in a heavy-bottomed medium saucepan, heat the corn syrup. Stir in the sugar and cook over moderately high heat, undisturbed, until a deep amber caramel forms, about 10 minutes. Remove from heat and stir in the butter. Stir in the cream in a thin stream. Transfer the caramel to a heatproof pitcher and allow to cool.

Pour caramel over each cheesecake and refrigerate. When ready to serve, sprinkle coarse salt over each cheesecake and top with mint sprigs. Makes 6 servings.

enjoy with

CAVE SPRING CELLARS
Dolomite Brut
www.cavespringtcellars.com

enjoy with

PONDVIEW ESTATE WINERY
Barrel Fermented Chardonnay
www.pondviewwinery.com

butternut squash pudding with maple cream

2 farm fresh eggs
1-1/2 cups (375 mL) butternut squash, cooked and mashed
3/4 cup (180 mL) packed brown sugar
1/2 teaspoon (2.5 mL) Ontario salt
1/2 teaspoon (2.5 mL) ground cinnamon
1-2/3 cups (400 mL) light cream
4 tablespoons (60 mL) sour cream
1 tablespoon (15 mL) Ontario maple syrup
1 tablespoon (15 mL) orchard walnuts, finely chopped

Preheat oven to 350F (180C). Beat the eggs in a large bowl. Add the squash, sugar, salt and cinnamon. Beat well. Gradually stir in cream. Pour into 8 - 6 ounce custard cups. Place cups in shallow baking pan and pour in enough hot water to come half way up sides of cups. Bake for 40 minutes or until knife inserted in centre comes out clean. Remove cups from water and set aside to cool. Mix the sour cream and maple syrup together. When puddings are cool, top with a dollop of maple sour cream and sprinkle with walnuts. Serves 8.

York Region

SOUTHBROOK PUMPKIN PATCH
Open from September to November, 10 to 6

Bill Redelmeier has a long tradition with farming. The original family farm was 1,000 acres before 3 generations split it among themselves so they could all continue to farm. Bill grew up on the Brook Farm and later acquired the South Farm and that is how the Southbrook name came to be. In 1984, Bill put a picnic table at the end of his farm laneway to see if anyone would buy the vegetables he put on it. Little did he realize how hungry city folk were for authentic farm and country experiences. Today the Southbrook Pumpkin Patch has parking for 800 to 1,000 cars and sells over 6,000 pies over the Thanksgiving weekend. It's one of our most popular farm and country traditions. www.southbrookpumpkinpatch.com

1150 Major Mackenzie Drive W, Richmond Hill

custard

1 1/2 cups (375 mL) whole milk
1 1/2 cups (375 mL) whipping cream
4 farm fresh egg yolks
1/2 cup (125 mL) sugar
1 teaspoon (5 mL) pure vanilla extract

Combine the milk and 1 cup (250 mL) of cream in a saucepan and warm over medium low heat. Meanwhile, combine egg yolks, sugar and remaining ½ cup (125 mL) cream in a bowl and whisk until lemony colour and thick.

When milk begins to form tiny bubbles around the edges of the pan, dribble a tiny amount into the egg mixture, whisking vigorously so the hot milk does not cook the eggs. Continue to dribble hot milk and whisk until half of the hot milk is used. Pour egg mixture into the remaining hot milk and whisk to combine. Using a wooden spoon, stir custard over low heat until thick enough to coat the back of the spoon and leaves a clear trail when a finger is drawn through it, about 6 minutes. Cool to room temperature, add vanilla.

Each dollar you spend on local food is a vote for the kind of culinary culture you want.

caramel ice cream

3/4 cup (180 mL) sugar, plus 2 tablespoons (30 mL)
2 tablespoons (30 mL) water
1 teaspoon (5 mL) Niagara verjus
1 cup (250 mL) whipping cream
4 farm fresh egg yolks
pinch of salt
1 1/2 cups (375 mL) whole milk
1 tablespoon (15 mL) pure vanilla extract

In a saucepan, combine the sugar, water and verjus. Cook over medium high heat, stirring with a wooden spoon until the sugar dissolves, about 1 to 2 minutes. Stop stirring and cook until the syrup is amber in colour, about 5 to 6 minutes, swirling it to ensure even cooking. Watch closely to avoid burning.

Remove from heat and carefully drizzle in 3/4 cup (180 mL) cream into the hot syrup. Be very careful, mixture will bubble vigorously. Stir with a wooden spoon until smooth. Place over medium low heat and cook until bubbles form around the edges of the pan, about 5 minutes.

Whisk yolks, salt, 2 tablespoons (30 mL) sugar and remaining cream in large bowl until lemony in colour. Whisk caramel mixture into egg yolks. Using a wooden spoon, stir custard over low heat until thick enough to coat the back of the spoon and leaves a clear trail when a finger is drawn through it, about 6 minutes. Remove from heat, stir in vanilla and pour custard into large bowl; refrigerate until completely cooled.

Pour custard into an ice cream maker and freeze according to manufacturer's instructions.

pastry for sweet applications

2 1/4 cups (560 mL) all-purpose flour, plus extra for dusting
1/2 cup (125 mL) icing sugar
1 cup (250 mL) country fresh butter, chilled
and cut into small cubes
2 farm fresh eggs, beaten
2 tablespoons (30 mL) whole milk

Whisk together the flour and icing sugar in a large bowl. Using a pastry blender, work the cubes of butter into the flour and sugar until you end up with a fine, crumbly mixture. Add the eggs and milk to the mixture and gently work it together until you have a ball of dough. Flour it lightly and pat it into a flat round. Wrap it in plastic wrap and refrigerate to rest for at least half an hour.

On a lightly floured surface, roll out the pastry to fit your tart pan. To make sure it is the right size, take your tart pan, flip it over, and place it on the rolled out pastry. The pastry should be about an inch larger than your pan.

When the pastry is rolled to the desired size, lightly roll pastry around your rolling pin, dusting off any excess flour as you roll. Unroll onto the top of your tart pan. Gently press pastry into bottom and up sides of pan, trim remaining pastry. Prick bottom of dough, cover and refrigerate for 20 minutes.

To prebake the tart shell, preheat oven to 375F (190C). Line the unbaked pastry shell with parchment paper or aluminum foil filled with pie weights. Bake for 35 to 40 minutes or until the crust is dry and lightly browned. Remove weights and cool crust on wire rack.

pastry for savoury applications

1 cup (250 mL) all-purpose flour, plus extra for dusting
1/2 cup (125 mL) country fresh butter,
chilled and cut into small pieces
1 teaspoon (5 mL) Ontario salt
1 farm fresh egg
1 tablespoon (15 mL) cold milk

Heap the flour on a work surface and make a well in the centre. Put the butter, salt and egg in a food processor and pulse until butter is the size of peas. Spoon the butter mixture into the flour well. Little by little, draw in the flour, working the dough delicately until it has a grainy texture. Add the milk and incorporate gently with your fingertips until the dough begins to hold together. Knead the dough 5 or 6 times, wrap in plastic and refrigerate for 30 minutes.

On a lightly floured surface, roll out the pastry to fit your tart pan. To make sure it is the right size, take your tart pan, flip it over, and place it on the rolled out pastry. The pastry should be about an inch larger than your pan.

When the pastry is rolled to the desired size, lightly roll pastry around your rolling pin, dusting off any excess flour as you roll. Unroll onto the top of your tart pan. Gently press pastry into bottom and up sides of pan, trim remaining pastry. Prick bottom of dough, cover and refrigerate for 20 minutes.

To prebake the tart shell, preheat oven to 375F (190C). Line the unbaked pastry shell with parchment paper or aluminum foil filled with pie weights. Bake for 35 to 40 minutes or until the crust is dry and lightly browned. Remove weights and cool crust on wire rack.

The Ontario Pantry

We all have food in our cupboards so why not buy Ontario products to stock it with? Throughout the province there are culinary entrepreneurs who are as passionate about creating foodstuffs as growers are about growing food.

The following is a list of suggested pantry items to help you cook local. I've also included websites whenever possible so you can shop through their websites. This is simply a start to the long list of Ontario's local products, so read labels and always ask for Ontario products when shopping. Check the ontariotable.com website for more of Ontario's delicious local products.

OILS

Who can cook without oils? I usually have 2 varieties of oil on hand, extra virgin and traditional; one for salads and the other for cooking. Pristine Gourmet (www.pristinegourmet.com) is a great source for extra virgin oils, both soy and canola. Ouellette Farms in Middleville is a great source for grape seed oil (www.ouellettefarm.com).

VINEGARS

Aceto Niagara (www.acetoniagara.com) produces icewine vinegar along with a complete line of 100% Ontario vinegars. Niagara Vinegars (www.niagaravinegars.com) makes a line of varietal vinegars under the label Essence of Niagara and it includes a balsamic vinegar – yum! A Blueberry Balsamic vinegar can be found at Ouellette Farms in Middlville (ouellettefarm.com). Mr. Vinegar (www.mrvinegar.ca) produces 2 types of honey vinegar and 2 types of maple syrup vinegar.

EGGS

Beautiful farm fresh eggs can be found at many farmers' markets and farm markets. When in a grocery store, please read the labels to make sure you're buying wholesome Ontario eggs.

SALT

Ontario produces salt from ancient sea beds far beneath the ground we walk on. Sifto Salt in Goderich and Windsor Salt in Windsor are large industrial sites and far from the romantic visualization of salt piles on a shoreline, but make no mistake the quality and flavour is superb. Don't stock your pantry with anything else.

FLOUR

Arva Flour (www.arvaflourmill.com), Oak Manor (www.oakmanorfarms.com) and Grass Roots Organics (www.saugeenspecialtygrains.ca) are great Ontario flour brands. They produce both organic and local flours in many varieties from all-purpose to spelt and whole wheat to rye. They also produce cereals, pearl barley and popcorn.

CANNED TOMATOES, BEANS AND OTHER VEGETABLES

The following companies can 100% Ontario products. Choose these brands knowing you're buying local food.

August's Harvest (www.augustharvest.com) offers organic Pickled Garlic Flowers.

Ontario Natural Food Coop (www.onfc.ca): crushed, diced or peeled whole tomatoes; dried herbs and Ontario organic tofu, firm and extra firm.

Sunshine Farms (www.picklesplease.ca) preserves fresh spring asparagus, beets, bread & butter pickles, fiery dills and zesty pickled carrots.

Alymer brand produced by Delmonte Canada (www.delmontecanada.com) includes all tomato products, sliced beets and whole potatoes.

The Garlic Box (www.thegarlicbox.com) preserves fresh Ontario garlic as well as many other gourmet items like Pickled Winter Garlic Cloves and Hot Pickled Garlic Cloves.

Thomas's Utopia (www.thomascanning.com) brand tomato products both organic and traditional.

Cottam Gardens (www.cottamgardens.com) tomato products as well as red kidney and black beans in a can.

ICE SYRUP

It's as rich as maple syrup, as fresh as grape juice and as complex as icewine. Ice syrup is a new invention from Niagara that is the perfect culinary ingredient. Use it for marinating, roasting, grilling, basting and even drizzling. It can even be used fresh from the bottle over top of ice cream. It's a fantastic multi-use culinary ingredient and a must-have for any kitchen (www.icesyrup.com).

DRIED FRUIT

Look for delicious dried cranberries from Bala while Cherry Lane (www.cherrylane.net) in Vineland offers dried cherries in their store. County Natural processes dried apples and dried pears that are crispy and work beautifully on a cheese platter in place of crackers. Reif Estate Winery dries Coronation Sovereign grapes into raisins.

JAM, JELLIES AND SWEET PRESERVES

Throughout the province at farm markets and farmers' markets you'll find many versions of jam, jellies and preserves made with fresh, ripe Ontario fruits. Like grapes into wine, making jams, jellies and preserves is an important way for farmers to add a new nonperishable product to what they currently offer their customers. They're like a taste of summer flavours in the dreary days of winter. Try them all and share your favourites.

VERJUS

Verjus is Ontario's answer to lemon juice. Use it in place of lemon juice in recipes, it will prevent oxidation on fruit, makes a delicious salad vinaigrette or dressing and is great on its own with soda water for a refreshing summertime spritzer. You'll find it at wineries like Featherstone or Crown Bench and Hughes Vineyard (Ed is a chef) in Beamsville makes it.

NUTS

Ontario grows Northern pecans, walnuts, chestnuts, peanuts and hazelnuts. Ontario is the largest producer of peanuts in Canada. For the best, look for Kernal Peanuts (www.canadianpeanuts.com) in Norfolk County and Picard Peanuts (www.picardspeanuts.ca).

SOY SAUCE

Yes we do make a great soy sauce in Ontario. Check out the brand, Pristine Gourmet Soy Sauce (www.pristinegourmet.com).

MAPLE SYRUP

Canada produces 80% of the world's maple syrup and Ontario produces the bulk of that; it's Ontario's quintessential food product. I certainly can't list all of the amazing producers here but I am sure you have a maple syrup producer not far from you. Check out some unique maple syrups like the Maple Icewine Syrup from Jackmans (www.themaplestore.co) or the ultra thick syrup from Stanley's Olde Maple Lane Farm (www.stanleysfarm.com) and the uber delicious maple products from Fulton's (www.fultonns.ca). Just make sure the label says Ontario maple syrup.

MUSTARDS

Most of Ontario's mustard seed comes from Saskatchewan. G. S. Dunn in Hamilton is the world's largest mustard mill. I was told an interesting story. Mustard seed from Saskatchewan, milled in Hamilton is purchased by a large French company, processed in France and sold back to Ontarians as French mustard. I say good for Canada for developing this amazing niche. As for the French (aka Canadian) mustard, true or not, what locavores should know is that Ontario no longer grows mustard seed so the closest producers are in Saskatchewan.

HONEY

Honey is grown in every corner of Ontario and sold at almost every farmers' market. Look for one next market day.

TOFU

All across the province you can find acres upon acres of soybeans and now a company is making Ontario tofu. Look for the Ontario Natural Food Coop brand (www.onfc.ca) in specialty food shops and some health food stores.

POPCORN

Ontario is Canada's largest producer of popping corn. The real fun is popping the corn when it's still on the cob! If you can't find any, try Uncle Bob's Popcorn (www.ontariopoppingcorn.com), they take web orders and White Meadow Farm (www.whitemeadowfarmas.com) for not only popping corn but this maple sugar farm makes a killer maple caramel corn.

CRACKERS

You'll find a few artisan cracker makers. Barrie Brothers (www.BarrieBrothers.com) make 2 wonderful crackers; stone wheat and vegetable with local ingredients. County Natural makes orchard designated fruit crackers with no sweeteners or preservatives. Monforte Dairy commissions a chef to make crackers from local ingredients.

GARLIC

More and more garlic producers are growing greater quantities of garlic to meet the growing demand. Convenient garlic in a jar is produced by August's Harvest (www.augustharvest.com) and The Garlic Box (www.thegarlicbox.com).

GRAPE JUICE

There are a few grape juice producers in the province. Look for Gesundheit (www.niagarajuicecompany.com) in the sexy, bright bottles. It comes in 2 flavours; vidal and baco noir. They're great for kids lunchboxes. Champanade (www.champanade.ca) is produced by Fermdale Vineyards in Beamsville. Frogpond Farm makes a delicious Chardonnay and Cabernet grape juice (www.frogpondfarm.ca).

CHEESE

Ontario was once a province that produced and exported cheese. Today, Ontario is giving birth to many new artisan cheesemakers who are producing some pretty exciting, unique and incredibly delicious cheeses. Kathy Guidi (www.artisancheesemarketing.com) and Guerth Pretty (www.cheeseofcanada.ca) are Ontario cheese experts and their websites and books should help you to find something new and scrumptious!

APPLE CIDER

Apple cider is Ontario's quintessential drink. During apple season, plastic jugs of the sweet juice show up at every farmers' market across the province. Some farmers store apples and continue to make apple cider long into the winter months. Celebrate it while you can.

DAIRY

From milk to yogurt, sour cream, butter, whipping cream and ice cream, we make it all here in Ontario from farm fresh Ontario milk. Please read the labels on the products you're buying to make sure you've got wholesome Ontario dairy.

CORNMEAL

Ontario produces massive amounts of wheat, corn and soy and now small artisans have taken some of the corn, both organic and traditional and are grinding it into cornmeal. It's beautiful and perfect for cornbreads (especially spiced with diced jalapeno peppers), polenta or for coating certain fish, poultry and meats. Oak Manor (www.oakmanorfarms.com) or Grass Roots Organics (www.saugeenspecialtygrains.ca) are great Ontario brands.

STOCKS AND SOUP

There is a soup company called Barrie Brothers (www.barriebrothers.com) that makes delicious soups and Ontario's Own (www.ontariosown.ca) that make a delicious chicken and vegetable stock.

RICE

Ontario doesn't grow white rice but it's rich in wild rice – which is actually a grass. Look for Manomi Wild Rice (www.canadianwildrice.com) and Black Duck Wild Rice from Curve Lake.

CURED MEATS

I found butchers across the province that take pride in making their own cured meat products. The variety often depended on the nationality of the butcher; great kielbassa from polish butchers; amazing salamis from German and super capicola from Italians. It reminds us how personal local food can get. There is one company that is king of the cured meats in Ontario; Pingue Prosciutto (www.pingueprosciutto.com) is available at specialty food shops.

FROZEN FRUIT AND VEGETABLES

Ontario is home to a large fiddlehead farm, Norcliff Farm. They sell fresh fiddleheads in season and frozen year round. Cherry Lane (www.cherrylane.net) in Vineland offer frozen orchard fruit and berries all year round. Thanks to a new freezing facility in Norfolk County, farmers across the province now have the ability to freeze their crops. For example, Mapleton Dairy is now freezing their crop of butternut squash.

DRIED BEANS

Look for the Thompson (www.thompsonslimited.com) label for Ontario dried red and white kidney beans, yellow eye beans and white pea beans (navy beans). There's an artisan farmer who grows a variety of beans and dries them under the label Hill Billy Beans, (www.hillbillybeans.com).

Like meat, fish and poultry that are available year round, most of these pantry foods are also available at any time of the year.

Just $10 a week creates
$2.4 billion a year!

Be part of the $10 a week
challenge and together we can
achieve the billion dollar impact.

Wine

Bill Redelmeier, proprietor of Southbrook Vineyards explains to a group of wine enthusiasts visiting his stunning winery, that there is really only one agricultural product that consumers would rather experience in a value added form – that's wine.

The Ontario wineries have grown in numbers as has the acreage of plump, juicy wine grapes. Each season in a vineyard has its own allure. Winter is pure magic with icewine, spring is filled with anticipation as the naked vines begin to sprout their greenery, summer is beguiling with rows upon rows of lush corduroy vineyards and just drive through any wine region in autumn, lift your nose and take a giant whiff. That's the seductive smell of sweet, ripe grapes ready to be fermented into some of the region's finest wines.

According to the Vintners Quality Alliance (VQA) there are 4 wine regions in Ontario; Lake Erie North Shore, Pelee Island, Niagara Peninsula, and the newest DVA (designated viticultural area) is Prince Edward County.

While this means these areas are geographically identified as ideal for the growing of wine grapes, it doesn't mean you won't find wineries beyond the borders of the four DVAs. Fruit wineries exist in every corner of the province and grape wineries are neatly tucked into warm weather pockets where you'd least expect them.

Get out there and try them all.
www.winesofontario.org
www.vqaontario.com
www.fruitwinesofontario.ca

Cheese

Ontario can claim a variety of artisanal fromageries from Upper Canada Cheese, Monforte Dairy and Fifth Town Cheese leading the way to amazing cheeses.

Each cheese company has unique characteristics all their own. Paron Cheese in Hannon is the only Ontario cheesemaker allowed to age its Italian-style cheeses on age worn wooden boards, Ces't Bon in St. Marys produces luscious cheese from their own herd of Toggenburg and LaMancha goats and Woolwich Dairy can be credited with introducing Ontarians to soft, creamy goat cheese. Each cheese made in Ontario comes with its own story, flavour and uniqueness.

While cows milk is the main staple for many cheeses, goat and sheep milk cheeses are becoming more popular as they offer different flavours and textures and delight the palates of cheese lovers across the province.

To have our artisanal fromageries grow and prosper we must all be on the lookout for these delicious cheeses and gobble them up – of course, whenever possible with a glass of delicious Ontario wine and some artisan crackers.

If you want to learn more about Ontario's artisanal cheeses, look for these great resources: Canadian Artisanal and Fine Cheese by Gurth Pretty and Canadian Cheese, a pocket Guide by Kathy Guidi www.artisancheesemarketing.com

Ontario Cheese Society
www.ontariocheese.org

> One of the very nicest things about life is the way we must regularly stop whatever it is we are doing and devote our attention to eating.
>
> Luciano Pavarotti

Buying Local

FOLLOW THE MONEY TRAIL

The local food movement sweeping the country is led by consumers and I think this is the very reason we face challenges such as lack of distribution and an agreed upon definition of local food. While there are great people working on distribution, what I can do is share my definition of local food so you may feel confident expanding your local food purchases.

For the most part, the search for local food started as a quest for safer and healthier food. There are others who buy local food for reasons of principle – environmental, animal welfare and sustainability. But the overarching priority is agricultural sustainability. It's the sustainability issue that deserves defining, for if we talk local but don't buy local, sustainability will never be achieved and we will lose our local food opportunities forever.

For this reason the definition of local food can only be judged by the bottom line dollar. By this I mean you must follow the money trail. If the money you're spending on local food stays in the hands of a local farmer, then that's sustainability. But if the money you spend on food locally goes to a company outside the province, then it's not sustainable.

Like the blood that trickles from a cut, our money bleeds out of our community if we're not conscious of our buying decisions. Let's stop the bleeding, make informed decisions and buy local. Read labels, ask for local food at the grocers and most importantly shop at farmers' markets and markets you find on farms.

So enjoy your lobster, coffee and chocolate for the pleasure they give, and then enjoy your ever-expanding purchases of local food with the satisfaction of knowing you're buying your way to a better food culture in Ontario.

Like the blood that trickles from a cut, our money bleeds out of our community if we're not conscious of our buying decisions.

If every household in Ontario spent just $10 of their grocery budget on local foods each week, there would be a $2.4 billion dollar influx into the provincial economy each year!

Where to buy local

AT A FARMERS' MARKET

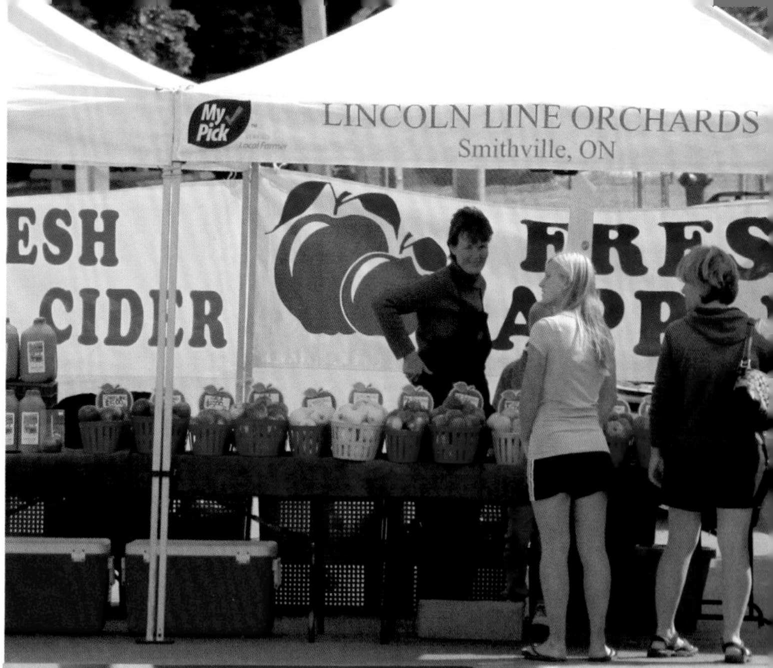

FARMERS' MARKETS ONTARIO®

Before there were supermarkets, people would congregate at a central meeting place to buy from local farmers bearing bushels of just-picked produce, as well as butchers and bakers offering their freshest wares. These marketplaces were the hearts and hubs of their communities: where neighbours would meet and mingle, socializing with each other and with the people producing their food. Today, farmers' markets perform the same role, bringing town and country together and ensuring easy access to nutritious locally grown food. But not all vendors are farmers, so look for the MyPick® Verified Local Farmer® symbol. It identifies real farmers who sell only what they grow. Today, farmers' markets are popping up all across Ontario, and they're still about connecting— to the land, to each other, and to a better quality of life. To find a market near you, visit the website.

www.farmersmarketsontario.com

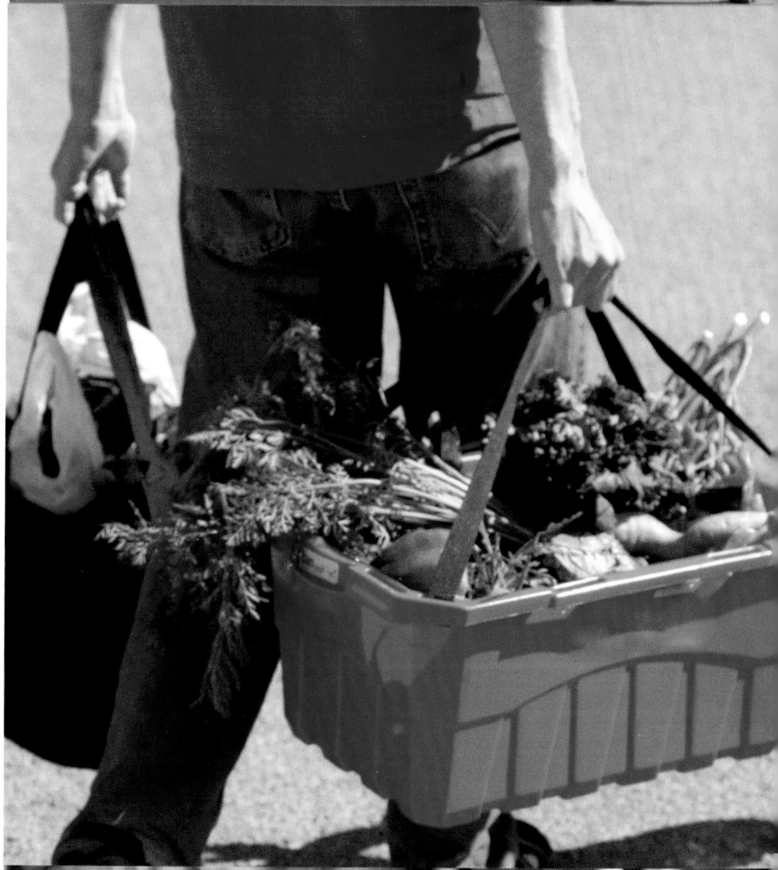

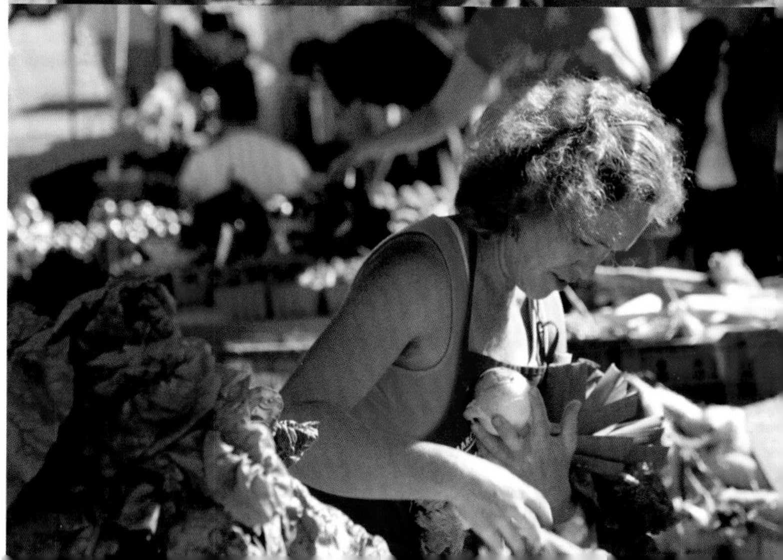

AT AN ON-FARM MARKET

ONTARIO FARM FRESH

There are plenty of on-farm markets tucked snugly among the orchards, gardens, fields, vineyards and backroads of Ontario. Some are as small as a wagon parked road-side with an honour box letting you know that trust in country living is noticeably different from city life. Others are beautifully restored barns that offer venues for weddings, theatre and parties. Large or small you will experience quintessential farm and country conviviality that is wholesome and nurturing to young and old alike. Visit one with the family and enjoy wagon rides and corn mazes; buy some naturally raised meats, a freshly baked pie or a jar of luscious honey; pick your own pumpkin and warm up to a steamy mug of cider or boiled ear of corn. Meet a farmer, taste his food and become part of your local food community. To find an on-farm market near you, visit the website.

www.ontariofarmfresh.com

We crave bright salads in the summer and savoury roasts in the winter. And when we do, Mother Nature provides us with the right ingredients at the right time.

Ontario Fruits & Vegetables
AVAILABILITY GUIDE

VEGETABLES	J	F	M	A	M	J	J	A	S	O	N	D
Artichoke								●	●	●		
Asian Vegetables						●	●	●	●	●	●	
Asparagus					●	●						
Beans (Green/Wax)						●	●	●	●	●		
Beets	●	●	●	●			●	●	●	●	●	●
Bok Choy						●	●	●	●	●	●	
Broccoli						●	●	●	●	●		
Brussels Sprouts									●	●	●	
Cabbage	●	●	●	●		●	●	●	●	●	●	●
Carrots	●	●	●	●	●		●	●	●	●	●	●
Cauliflower						●	●	●	●	●	●	
Celery							●	●	●	●		
Corn							●	●	●	●		
Cucumbers (Field)						●	●	●	●	●		
Cucumbers (Greenhouse)	●	●	●	●	●	●	●	●	●	●	●	●
Eggplant								●	●	●		
Garlic	●	●					●	●	●	●	●	●
Leeks	●	●						●	●	●	●	●
Lettuce (Assorted)						●	●	●	●	●		
Lettuce (Greenhouse)	●	●	●	●	●	●	●	●	●	●	●	●
Mushrooms	●	●	●	●	●	●	●	●	●	●	●	●
Onions (Cooking)	●	●	●	●	●	●	●	●	●	●	●	●
Onions (Green)						●	●	●	●	●	●	
Onions (Red)	●	●	●						●	●	●	●
Parsnips	●	●	●	●				●	●	●	●	●
Peas (Green)						●	●					
Peas (Snow)						●	●	●	●			
Peppers (Field)							●	●	●	●		
Peppers (Greenhouse)			●	●	●	●	●	●	●	●	●	●
Potatoes	●	●	●				●	●	●	●	●	●
Radicchio						●	●	●				
Radishes					●	●	●	●	●	●	●	
Rapini							●	●	●	●		
Rutabaga	●	●	●	●	●	●	●	●	●	●	●	●
Spinach					●	●	●	●	●	●		
Sprouts	●	●	●	●	●	●	●	●	●	●	●	●
Squash	●	●	●					●	●	●	●	●
Sweet Potatoes	●	●	●	●	●	●	●	●	●	●	●	●
Tomatoes (Field)							●	●	●	●		
Tomatoes (Greenhouse)			●	●	●	●	●	●	●	●	●	●
Zucchini							●	●	●	●		

FRUITS	J	F	M	A	M	J	J	A	S	O	N	D
Apples	●	●	●	●	●	●		●	●	●	●	●
Apricots							●	●				
Blueberries							●	●	●			
Cherries						●	●					
Crabapples									●	●	●	
Cranberries										●		
Currants (Red/Black)							●	●				
Gooseberries							●	●				
Grapes								●	●			
Muskmelon								●	●			
Nectarines								●	●			
Peaches							●	●	●			
Pears								●	●	●	●	●
Plums							●	●	●	●		
Raspberries							●	●	●			
Rhubarb	●	●	●	●	●	●						
Strawberries						●	●					
Strawberries (Day Neutral)					●	●	●	●	●	●		
Watermelon							●	●	●			

Note: Availability dates may change by several weeks with respect to rare varieties and/or weather conditions.

Resources

ONTARIO'S MOST DELICIOUS MAPS

Use these maps to start your own local food journey. Take The Ontario Table book, pack up the family and spend the day enjoying some farm and country conviviality.

Buy Algoma Eat Fresh
www.buyalgoma.ca

Bountiful Brant
www.bountifulbrant.com

Eat Local Caledon
www.eatlocalcaledon.org

Chatham Kent Buy Local Buy Fresh
www.buylocalbuyfreshchathamkent.com

The Hills of Headwaters, Dufferin
www.thehillsofheadwaters.com

Durham Farm Fresh
www.durhamfarmfresh.ca

Savour Elgin
www.savourelgin.ca

Essex County Federation of Agriculture
www.ecfa.ca

Frontenac Local Flavours
www.localflavours.org

Food Link Grey Bruce
www.foodlinkgreybruce.com

Guelph Wellington Local Food
www.guelphwellingtonlocalfood.ca

Harvest of Haldimand
www.harvestofhaldimand.com

Simply Local Halton
www.halton.ca

Hamilton Eat Local
www.environmenthamilton.org

Harvest Hastings
www.harvesthastings.ca

Holland Marsh Gold
www.hollandmarshgold.com

Huron Perth Farm to Table
www.huronperthfarmtotable.ca

Kawartha Choice Farm Fresh
www.kawarthachoice.com

Kent Federatiaon of Agricultlure
www.ofa.on.ca

Food Down the Road, Kingston
www.fooddowntheroad.ca

Locally Lambton
www.locallylambton.com

Lanark Local Flavour
www.lanarklocalflavour.ca

London Middlesex Local Food Guide
www.middlesextourism.ca

Apple Pie Trail, Muskoka
www.applepietrail.ca

Savour Muskoka
www.savourmuskoka.com

Niagara Culinary Trail
www.niagaraculinarytrail.com

Norfolk Farms
www.norfolkfarms.com

Local Food Northumberland
www.northumberlandcounty.ca

Farmers' Markets Ontario
www.farmersmarketsontario.com

Foodland Ontario
www.foodland.gov.on.ca

Fruit Wines of Ontario
www.fruitwinesofontario.ca

Greenbelt Fresh, Ontario
www.greenbeltfresh.ca

Home Grown Ontario
www.homegrownontario.ca

Local Food Plus, Ontario
www.localfoodplus.ca

Local Harvest, Ontario
www.localharvest.ca

Ontario CSA Directory
www.csafarms.ca

Ontario Farm Fresh
www.ontariofarmfresh.com

Savour Ontario
www.savourontario.ca

Resources

ONTARIO'S MOST DELICIOUS MAPS

Sustain Ontario
www.sustainontario.com

The Ontario Table
www.ontariotable.com

Wines of Ontario
www.winesofontario.ca

Ontario Berries
www.ontarioberries.com

Ontario Culinary Tourism Alliance
www.ontarioculinary.com

Ontario Fresh
www.ontariofresh.ca

Savour Ottawa
www.savourottawa.ca

Buy Local Oxford
www.oxfordbuylocal.ca

Grown in Peel
www.peelregion.ca

Peterborough & Kawartha
www.visitourtable.com

Harvest in the County, Prince Edward County
www.harvestin.ca

Rainy River Buy Local Buy Fresh
www.foodlink.ca

Simcoe County Farm Fresh
www.simcoecountyfarmfresh.com

Slow Food Superior
www.slowfoodsuperior.ca

Savour Stratford
www.savourstratford.com

Eat Local Sudbury
www.eatlocalsudbury.com

Thunder Bay Country Market
www.thunderbaycountrymarket.com

Foodlink Waterloo Region
www.fooklink.ca

York Region Food Network
www.yrfn.ca

Declare Yourself a Local Food Champion!

Take a photograph of yourself on your favourite farm with your copy of The Ontario Table and send it to www.ontariotable.com. We will post it on the website and declare you as one of the growing number of consumers spending $10 a week on local food. Together we're building stronger communities, sustainable agriculture and a better food world.

Do it today! Attend a peach harvest, strawberry tea, pancake breakfast, melon festival, mushroom hunt or county fair and become part of your food culture.

Farmer Index

This book is dedicated to the farmers who risk it all to make our lives more delicous.

Recipe Index

After only two years of travelling Ontario for local foods, I can't profess to know all there is to know about Ontario's local food. Far from it. I've just skimmed the surface. What I have learned is that there is much more to discover, plenty more to taste and endless opportunities to eat. I do however, feel very comfortable and entrenched in the conviviality of Ontario's farming country and its people; it has become my new home away from home. Join me in making it yours too.

To be continued…

www.ontariotable.com